WOMEN'S ROAD TO ROCK GUITAR

Express Yourself by Learning How to Play Lead & Rhythm Guitar

NIKKI O'NEILL

Alfred Music
P.O. Box 10003
Van Nuys, CA 91410-0003
alfred.com

ISBN-10: 0-7390-9954-X (Book & CD)
ISBN-13: 978-0-7390-9954-4 (Book & CD)

Cover Photos
Photo of Nikki O'Neill: © Larry Lytle • Photo of Marshall Amps: courtesy of Marshall Amplification

Contents

Acknowledgements

I'd like to thank everybody who believed in me and helped make this book possible. I dedicate it to the love of my life: my incredible husband and musical partner Rich Lackowski, who never stops believing in me, my gifts or my ability to accomplish all the goals that I envision. While the road to accomplishing some of these goals often features hurdles that could trigger insecurities in any artist, he continues to show me his love and support, no matter what.

Thanks to my mother and grandmother, who both happen to be named Krystyna and grew up in Russia and Poland. With their experiences with war and suppressive regimes, they never got to fulfill their dreams of taking music lessons. My grandmother had begun playing the guitar, but the two World Wars basically tore her family apart, and she never got to play again. In my mother's hometown, local representatives for the Communist regime, who saw music education as a bourgeoisie activity, scared her into quitting her piano lessons. I feel incredibly lucky that I got to grow up in a place and time where I've been able to pursue my lifelong dedication to music, and make a career out of playing my guitar.

To my father Frank (RIP) who maybe wasn't quite as into screaming hard rock guitars as I was, but I still thank him for driving me to my first guitar workshop and for buying me my first pedal. Mom, dad, and grandmother…I love you all.

Thanks to my friends and everyone that I've had the joy of creating music with, including Joshua "Cartier" Cutsinger, Ed Lyon, Nikki Perry, Sean Young, Harold Branch, Lisa Swarbrick, Paul Kezmarsky, Russell Booker, Alan Gottesman, Yoshi Takemasa, Harel Shachal, Heberson Vieira Da Costa, and Hermes "Tuco" Vieira Da Costa. My gratitude also goes out to the many guitar players mentioned in this book who lit the spark in me, motivated me to pick up the guitar and provided my life with a sense of wonder, romance, power, confidence, and possibility.

I extend a very special thanks to the entire team at Alfred Music and Daisy Rock Guitars, including Ron Manus, Tish Ciravolo, Link Harnsberger, Nat Gunod, Holly Fraser, Ted Engelbart, Antonio Ferranti, Donny Trieu, Jared Meeker, Alex Ordonez, Billy Lawler, and Danielle Braus; photographer Larry Lytle; Evan Skopp at Seymour Duncan; Jillian Jepsen at The Museum of Making Music; Lise Axelson at ELLA; Fred Winston at New School University; my teachers Elisabeth Fridén, Perry Stenbäck, Hasse Lindén, Zak Keith, Quint Starkie, Johannes Kjellberg, Leon Kaleta Ligan-Majek and George from Ghana, Steve Tarshis, Glenn Alexander, Jean Marc Belkadi, Vadim Zilbershtein, and Fred Sokolow.

Another very special thank you goes out to Jennifer Batten, Kat Dyson, Sue Foley, Lita Ford, Kaki King, Ann Klein, Bibi McGill, Orianthi Panagaris, Vicki Peterson, Ana Popovic, and Nancy Wilson for sharing your inspirational advice and perspectives throughout the book. Much love and respect goes out to you!

Finally, my gratitude goes out to guitarists extraordinaire Will Ray, Frank Simes, Jennifer Batten, and Sue Foley, who took the time to give me career advice; the fans of my video guitar lessons: and last but not least, my students; you all make my life beautiful, full of purpose, and a lot more fun, and I'm deeply grateful to you for that.

Track 1 An MP3 CD is included with this book. Using the disc will help make learning more enjoyable and the information more meaningful. Listening to the tracks on the CD will help you correctly interpret the rhythms and feel of each example. The symbol to the left appears next to each song or example that is performed on the CD. The track number below each symbol corresponds directly to the song or example you want to hear. Track 1 will help you tune to this CD.

Why a Rock Guitar Book for Women?

First of all, thanks for picking up this book! I truly believe that playing rock guitar is one of the coolest ways you can express yourself.

With this book, I want to help you: broaden your rock rhythm and lead guitar skills, get familiar with the basics on amps and effects, understand rock song structures, and gain a few other useful skills needed to play on your own or in a band. My intention is to encourage *your* creativity so that you have a good palette for expressing yourself. I also want to help you avoid obstacles that could slow your growth.

These topics, of course, also apply to men who want to play guitar. So why a rock guitar book for women?

Well, I also want to make you aware that you're part of a cool but rarely acknowledged community. When *Rolling Stone* magazine lists the 100 most important guitarists of all time, they usually only include two or three women. Many male guitarists or teachers don't think about mentioning the great female players that are out there. Few realize that some of the first pioneers of the electric guitar were women. In this book, you'll find the learning experiences and playing advice from some world-class female guitarists, including Jennifer Batten, Kat Dyson, Sue Foley, Lita Ford, Kaki King, Ann Klein, Bibi McGill, Orianthi Panagaris, Vicki Peterson, Ana Popovic, and Nancy Wilson.

Also, some girls and women who sign up for guitar classes often find the vibe a little intimidating because soloing, technique, and gear—topics which many guys can debate for hours—can seem mystifying. I want to demystify these things for you. While becoming a great guitar player does take work (I won't lie about that!), it's also a lot of fun and very empowering. With this book, I want to make your experience of learning rock guitar fun and exciting.

It also includes a list of essential recordings by female electric guitar pioneers like Memphis Minnie; influential all-girl bands like The Runaways, and excellent lead guitarists of today like Orianthi Panagaris and Ana Popovic. It's impossible to cover everyone deserving of mention, but hopefully the list will provide a unique rock guitar history lesson and lots of inspiration!

Today, there are great female guitarists in every genre of rock. As I started writing this book, hard rock icon Alice Cooper hired guitarist Orianthi Panagaris to play on his tour, TV commercials and billboard ads started featuring young women playing electric guitars, and girly pop teen idols are now strumming guitars on stage and in music videos. As a result, I've seen a clear increase in the number of female guitar students, and many of these girls—some as young as seven years old—are showing up to class with electric guitars. Guitar companies like Daisy Rock Guitars are making guitars that are easier for girls to play, guitar stores are hiring more women, and bands are more open to recruiting female guitar players. This is a great cultural change.

This book moves quickly and is best used with a teacher. There is no substitute for a good teacher who can watch and listen to you play. If you use this book without a teacher, take your time and be sure you are able to play each example smoothly and evenly before moving on.

Do I Need to Read Music to Use This Book?

You don't need to read music to use this book. The tracks on the accompanying MP3 CD will let you hear demonstrations of the examples and exercises. Many of these are in the styles of very influential rock songs that have stood the test of time. If you're very new to the guitar you can choose to start with Appendix B: Quick Review of the Basics starting on page 137 of the book. It covers everything from open chords to basic rhythm and, if you're interested, you can learn to read music there, too.

Use this book as a guide as you're jamming together with friends and taking lessons with a teacher. If you don't have jamming buddies or a teacher for now, use this book on your own and jam along with recordings of your favorite bands!

Things You Should Know Before Diving In
- How to identify the six guitar strings by number and locate the first fret
- How to comfortably play full open-position chords on guitar, including F major

If you're not there yet, be very patient with yourself as the book isn't directed towards total beginners. You'll find a quick review of the basics in the back that will get you up to speed and ready to learn from this book.

If you have an acoustic guitar: Be patient with yourself as you learn to play the examples. An acoustic guitar usually has a wider neck and much thicker strings than an electric guitar, which may add some difficulty. Go easy on any string-bending licks.

If you're a total beginner: Start with the basics in Appendix B (page 137). Play the book examples with open chords and power chords instead of barre chords. Don't overdo your practice! A short but consistent practice of 15–30 minutes per day will help your hands get used to the stretches.

If you're a more experienced guitarist: You'll learn about song structures in rock, soloing across the neck with three fundamental rock scales (major, natural minor, and minor pentatonic), rock and blues lead guitar licks, rhythm guitar techniques, chord types and strum patterns, basic fretboard navigation, contemporary lead guitar techniques, and the basics of effects pedals and amps. You'll also get practice tips and other playing-related advice.

If you're a teacher: This book is for teen and adult players. Since it's a method book, the content is laid out in a progressive order. Make sure to use additional and complimentary materials to your lessons that cover full songs, ear training and music theory, sightreading, rhythm work, playing technique, and other areas more substantially.

Are you ready? Let's get started!

Photo by Laurel Geare

Nikki O'Neill

Section 1:
The Defining Moment — Knowing Your Guitar

THE PARTS OF YOUR ELECTRIC GUITAR

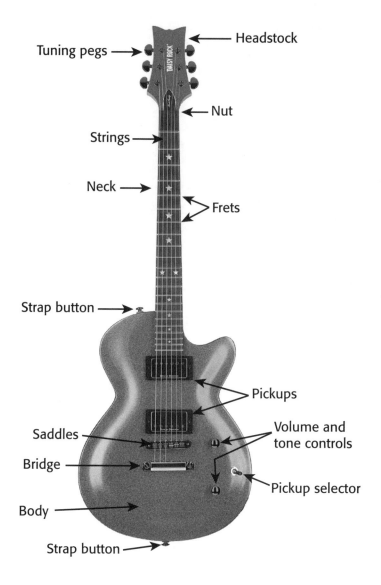

Tuning pegs
Headstock
Nut
Strings
Neck
Frets
Strap button
Pickups
Saddles
Volume and tone controls
Bridge
Pickup selector
Body
Strap button

Pickups — How They Shape Your Tone

When you strum the strings, their vibration generates a small electric current in the *pickups* of your guitar. Pickups contain magnets wrapped with coils of very thin metal wire. The current moves through these coils; then your guitar cable, into your amp… and out through your amp's speaker comes your music!

The two most common pickup types are *single coils* and *humbuckers* (*double-coils*). Humbuckers were invented to prevent unwanted humming sounds, and also tend to have a fatter tone. Both types sound great in different ways and contribute to creating a guitar player's signature sound.

Humbucker pickup

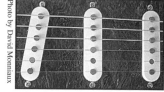

Single coil pickups

Your guitar has a three-way or five-way *pickup selector switch*. It lets you switch between your different pickup sounds. You can replace the pickups to change your guitar's sound. A guitarist's sound, however, really comes first from their fingers and how they play; then comes the combination of guitar and amp.

Choosing Your Strings

Electric guitars use steel strings. The *gauge* tells how thick they are. The most common gauges for rock guitar are .009s, .010s, and .011s. If you have small hands or are new to rock-style string bends, start with the .009s. Heavier strings create a fuller sound, but are more difficult to play.

If you play music with dropped guitar tunings, use heavier strings to keep them at a good tension, but make sure to take your guitar to an instrument shop to get the intonation adjusted. This way, the new gauge (and resulting change of tension) won't put too much stress on the guitar neck.

HOLDING YOUR GUITAR

As female players, we often play guitars that are heavy in proportion to our frame. If they also have a wide neck or hang really low at knee level (for the rock star look), this makes playing more challenging too. Take a moment to look at these pictures and read the quick tips on how to play correctly, so that you can avoid strains and injuries.

Sitting

Don't play like the couch potato in the picture with the guitar laying flat down across your lap! It makes your fingers very restricted. You'll play better if you and your guitar sit up straight.

Good sitting position

Bad sitting position

Standing

If you plan to perform live, where you sing and play simultaneously or play with a band, you should stand up when you practice as much as you can. Some guitarists like to wear their guitar very low, while others wear it higher (for greater ease of playing). Find out what strap length works best for you.

Plugging In

To avoid accidentally stepping on your cable and yanking it out, lead the cable through the strap before you plug it in.

Standing

Lead the cable through the strap

Straps and Strap-Locks

Keep your strap on when you're sitting down, so that you don't have to think about holding the guitar in place while you're playing.

If you find your guitar strap coming off your guitar when you stand, invest in a strap-lock system. You can get it at any instrument shop; it doesn't cost much, and it will save you the stress.

Strap and strap lock

FINGERS, STRINGS, AND FRETS

Your left-hand fingers are numbered one through four. Your index finger is the 1st finger, your pinky, or little finger, is the 4th finger.

The frets are numbered starting from the nut (see page 7). The strings are numbered starting from the skinniest, highest-sounding string. If you're holding your guitar properly, the *1st string* is the string closest to the floor, and the *6th string* is the thickest, lowest-sounding string, which is closest to the ceiling.

Notice the fretboard diagram on the right, below. Diagrams such as this can be used to easily illustrate where to put your fingers to play.

Left-hand fingers

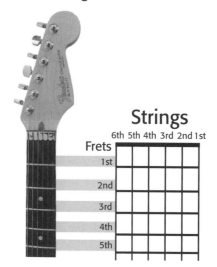

HOW TO READ CHORD DIAGRAMS

Fingering diagrams show where to place the fingers of your left hand. Strings not played are shown with dashed lines. The number within the circle indicates the finger that is pressed down.

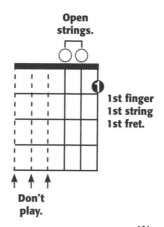

THE LEFT HAND *

You control a lot of your expressiveness on the guitar through string bends, vibrato, hammer-ons, pull-offs, trills, slides and other left-hand techniques. The left hand is also responsible for much of your speed, agility, and accuracy. So if you want your ideas to come out like you're imagining them, you need good left-hand chops. It isn't hard to achieve!

Placing Your Finger on the String

Press your fingertip as close to the fret wire as you can without being right on it. This placement will give you the best tone. Curl your fingers so that *only the tips of your fingers touch the strings.*

Finger placement

Keep the Fingers Curved

Keep your fingers curved and close to the fretboard and make sure that your fingertips aren't accidently touching any adjacent strings. This will allow you to play more fluidly and effortlessly.

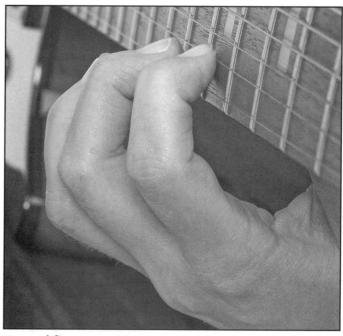

Curved finger position

* Left-handed players can reverse the instructions. When the book addresses the left hand, simply apply it to your right hand.

Wrist Position

It's very important not to bend your left wrist too much when you play. It can be tempting to do that to make certain chords easier to play, but it will fatigue your hand. Practice in front of a mirror and watch your wrist. It should definitely not be bent in a 90-degree angle! Keep it fairly straight and relaxed.

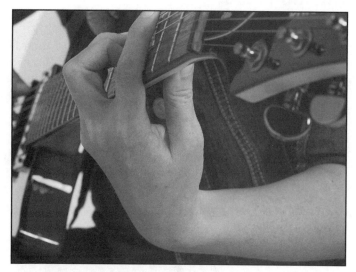

Don't bend the wrist too much

Thumb Position

Keep your thumb out of sight, resting on the back of the neck. You might see a lot of rock guitarists wrap their thumbs around the neck, but keeping your thumb behind the neck will make your fingers feel much less restricted. Your thumb should sit opposite the top joints of your index and middle fingers.

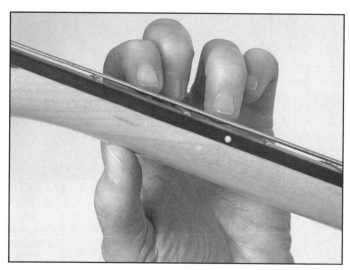

Thumb position

THE RIGHT HAND

It's your right hand that actually sounds most of the notes. To easily play the ideas you're hearing in your mind, a solid right-hand technique is needed. This will enable you to: play strums and other rhythm parts with ease, groove, and flow; control which strings will be heard; and regulate your volume, attack and tone. Great right-hand chops will also give you the agility to play quicker or busier music.

Right-Hand Position

Hold the pick firmly between your thumb and index finger. The pointy part of the pick makes contact with the strings. Keep your wrist and arm relaxed. The picking motion should come from just your wrist, not your entire arm. A *downstroke* is a downward sweeping motion toward the floor. An *upstroke* is an upward motion away from the floor.

Right arm position

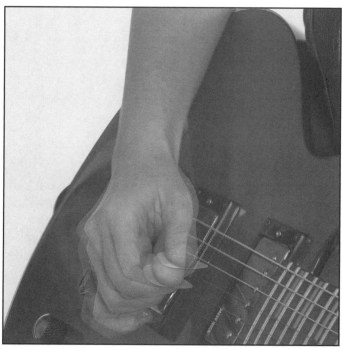

The picking motion is small, and from the wrist

Picks

Picks come in different sizes and gauges (thicknesses). Start out with a basic, medium-sized, medium-gauge pick. Really thin and flimsy picks are better for an acoustic guitar and are not great for electric guitars. Some picks have a matte finish (to help you control your grip), while others are more glossy. As you get more playing experience, experiment with different picks, as they provide the cheapest and easiest way to change your sound.

> "I use a tiny Fender heavy pick. I try to squeeze the most of it by using pinch harmonics, sweep picking, scraping the strings, and something I've started to do a bit for a change in texture is to really pound the pick right next to the bridge when pedaling the same note."
>
> **Jennifer Batten**, *guitarist and composer (Michael Jackson, Jeff Beck, solo artist)*

Photo by Cheryl Gorski

"I love switching between the pick and fingerpicking: I'll play a note (heavy attack with the pick) and then flip the pick between my thumb and palm to fingerpick a few notes. Quickly changing between polished notes and a raw bluesy attack with fingerpicking creates a great effect. It's almost like using two different guitars…

I use Fender heavy picks and my attack on the strings is hard for all the blues, rock or funk solos. When I want to play fast jazzy licks, my attack on the strings is light, barely touching them."

Ana Popovic, *blues guitarist, singer and songwriter*

DOWNSTROKES, UPSTROKES, AND ALTERNATE PICKING

You'll strum chords or play single notes by moving your pick in either a downstroke or upstroke motion. Here are the standard symbols for picking:

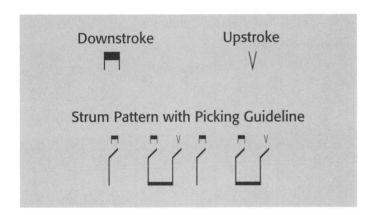

The symbols underneath the picking symbols on the left are called *rhythmic notation*. This is explained on page 14.

Alternate picking means that you continually move your pick down, up, down, up, etc. This is the technique that you'll be using for most of the examples in the book. Make sure that your upstrokes match the volume and tone quality of your downstrokes.

Only picking with downstrokes can create a bold and aggressive sound, which is very useful in some cases. But if you play a fast song and only use downstrokes, it will sound choppy and you won't be able to play it very quickly.

Picking choices are rarely random; the way you pick can greatly affect your speed, fluidity, rhythmic flow, and overall feel. You'll get to practice your picking technique by playing lots of cool strum patterns and lead guitar parts in this book. Make sure you follow the picking guidelines in the examples, and you'll sound like a pro!

The Big Question: Do I Really Have to Play with a Pick?

The pick gives a certain crispness and edge to your sound, compared to soft, fleshy fingers picking the strings, which sound quieter. You have to use a pick for certain techniques, such as tremolo and sweep picking in rock and metal, country-style guitar solos, or funk rhythm playing. It's wise to start out playing with a pick. Then, if you choose to skip it when you get more experienced, it should be a conscious decision— not because you thought it was difficult when you were a beginner.

So…are you ready to expand your rock rhythm guitar skills? Plug in and get ready!

To Start Rockin', You Need to Know...

TABLATURE (TAB)

Tablature (TAB) is a system of notation that graphically represents the strings and frets of the guitar fingerboard. Each note is indicated by placing a number, which indicates the fret to play, on the appropriate string.

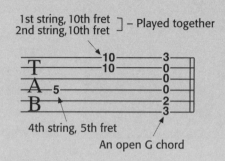

1st string, 10th fret ⌉ – Played together
2nd string, 10th fret ⌋

4th string, 5th fret

An open G chord

TIME SIGNATURES

Every piece of music has numbers at the beginning that tell us how to count time called *time signatures*. The top number represents the number of *beats* per measure. A beat is the basic measure of musical time. The bottom number represents the type of note receiving one count.

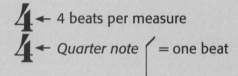

← 4 beats per measure

← *Quarter note* = one beat

THE STAFF AND CLEF

The staff has five lines and four spaces, which are read from left to right. At the beginning of the staff is a *clef*. Guitar music is written in *treble clef* which is sometimes called the *G clef*.

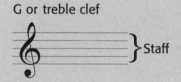

G or treble clef

Staff

RHYTHMIC NOTATION

Rhythmic notation is common in guitar music. It is a system of slash marks with stems and beams that notate specific *rhythms* (patterns of long and short sounds and silences) without specific *pitches* (pitch is the degree of highness or lowness of a musical sound). Rhythmic notation is usually used to show a rhythm guitar part.

Starting on page 17 where you will read your first examples, you'll find similar rhythmic notation above the TAB.

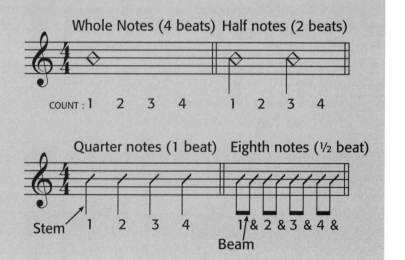

Whole Notes (4 beats) Half notes (2 beats)

COUNT : 1   2   3   4   1   2   3   4

Quarter notes (1 beat) Eighth notes (½ beat)

Stem   1   2   3   4   1 & 2 & 3 & 4 &

Beam

Good luck on your journey. Take your time with each lesson and be sure to be comfortable with the techniques before moving to the next lesson. Now let's get started playing rhythm guitar!

Section 2:
Rock Rhythm Guitar — The Essential Skills

TWO RHYTHM GUITARISTS,
TWO DIFFERENT ROCK AESTHETICS

The way you play your guitar is like an extension of your personality. Joan Jett and PJ Harvey are two rhythm guitarists who also are singers and songwriters who front their own bands. Although their styles of music and image are very different, they're both undeniably rock 'n' roll.

Joan Jett

Photo by Neil Zlozower/atlasicons

Rhythm guitar is all about providing the feel of the music. When playing rhythm guitar, we play riffs and strum chords to back up singers and lead guitarists. But even more importantly, together with the drummer and the bass player, rhythm guitarists create the drive behind the music. When people dance or tap their feet to the music, it's because of what's happening in the *rhythm section*, which often features the rhythm guitar.

Lead guitar playing is often about *improvisation*, which is the spontaneous composition of melodies. Using a variety of musical tools and guitar techniques at our disposal, which you will learn about later in this book, we thrill the listener by pouring our hearts out through creating something new, on the spot, and in the moment.

Born in Philadelphia, PA, on September 22, 1958, Joan Jett was a founding member of The Runaways, which was one of the first all-female hard rock bands that toured the world in the 1970s. She got her first Silvertone guitar and a chord book at age 13 and taught herself to play along with records. When she relocated to Los Angeles as a teen, she was heavily influenced by English glam-rock. Later on, punk became a great inspiration for her.

She has described herself as a "barre-chord basher", but is known as a very solid rhythm guitar player with great feel.

Once The Runaways broke up, she started her own label, Blackheart Records, and launched a very successful solo career with the classic single "I Love Rock 'n' Roll." She still records and tours actively, and is a huge inspiration for later generations of female rockers like L7 and Bikini Kill. In 2010, her early career was portrayed in Floria Sigismondi's movie, *The Runaways*.

PJ Harvey

Photo by George Chin/iconicpix/atlasicons

Born in Bridport, Dorset in England on October 9,1969, Polly Jean Harvey is considered by many to be "the queen of indie rock," with critically acclaimed albums like *Rid Of Me*, *Stories From the City, Stories From the Sea*, and *Let England Shake*.

Growing up on a sheep farm, her earliest influences were blues artists, '80s synth pop, new wave, art rock and American punk artists. On her first albums, her guitar style has a raw blues-punk feel, with jagged riffs mirroring her brutally honest lyrics. She doesn't like to repeat herself so she often switches styles and experiments with electronica, folk, pop, and indie rock.

Besides singing and playing guitar she plays saxophone, keyboards, percussion, and autoharp. She has said that she often doesn't touch an instrument for years unless she's recording or performing, which creates the need for her to relearn them.

MEASURES AND THE DOUBLE BAR LINE

Music notes are grouped together into groups of beats that are called *measures* or *bars*. The bars are indicated on the TAB by vertical lines called *bar lines*.

The *double bar line* is used to mark the end of a song or a section of a song. A section can be an *intro*, *verse*, *pre-chorus*, *chorus*, *bridge*, *guitar solo*, or another part of a song. We'll discuss song parts in detail in Section 4.

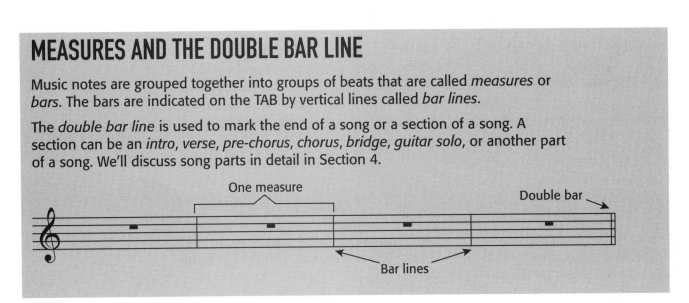

Power Chords — The Sound of Rock

Power chords are a crucial part of rock rhythm guitar playing. Once you learn one power chord, you can move it around, up and down the neck, to create different chords.

Two Strings. Two Notes. Two Frets Apart.

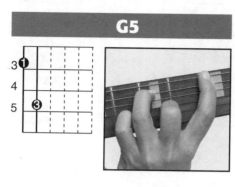

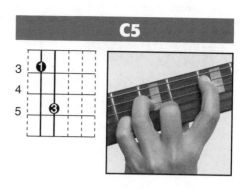

Power chords are also called *5 chords* (we'll explain why on page 20). Let's play the G5 chord just like the photo above. Place your 1st finger on the 6th string, 3rd fret. Add your 3rd finger to the 5th string, 5th fret. Hit the two notes at the same time. There's your G chord—rock style!

The C5 chord also starts at the 3rd fret, but is played on the 4th and 5th strings instead of the 5th and 6th. (Don't play the sixth string, as the chord won't sound right.) Note that both of these power chord shapes are *moveable*, which means they can be played on any fret (but the chord names will change when you move them).

 BABY, YOU GOT ME

Track 2

Try this power chord riff in the style of The Kinks' "You Really Got Me." Pay attention to the lowest fret fingered for each chord, and which two strings are played. Notice we are using the G5 shape you learned but at the 5th fret, which creates an A5.

If you are not used to reading TAB and don't read music, play along with the CD track to get the rhythm.

The *repeat sign* means to play the example again.

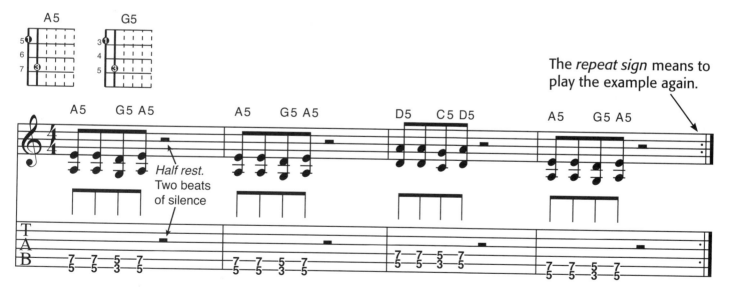

Most power chords have the shape we just learned. The following chords, however, are different.

POWER CHORDS WITH OPEN STRINGS

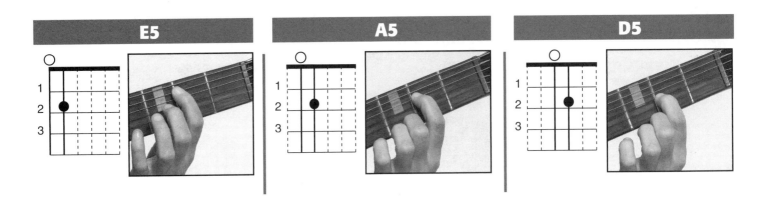

These versions of E5, A5 and D5 are not movable because they each include an open string:

- The E5 chord includes the open 6th string, which is a low E note*.
- The A5 chord has the open 5th string which is a low A note.
- The D5 chord includes the open 4th string, which is a low D note.

 RUNAWAY NIGHTS

Track 3

Try playing this chord progression in the style of The Runaways' "American Nights." You'll play the A5, D5, and E5 chords that all include open strings (use the chords at the top of this page).

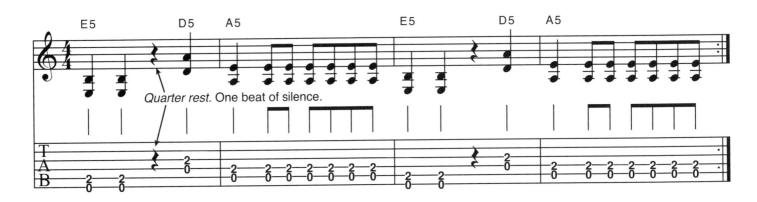

Quarter rest. One beat of silence.

* All musical notes are given a letter name from the musical alphabet, which is A B C D E F G.

A RAW, EDGY SOUND

Power chords sound very direct. They have more rawness and edge than other types of chords. That's because they're played on only two or three strings—usually the lowest strings: the 6th, 4th, and 3rd. This makes them sound tighter than *barre chords* (chords where the 1st finger covers all the strings) or *open chords* (chords played in the first few frets that include open strings). They're perfect for when you don't want lots of open strings ringing because you're playing a loud or fast rock tune with *distortion*.

Because power chords include fewer strings, you have to do a much smaller strumming motion with your pick. To get the right sound, you want the pick to hit just the two or three strings of the chord—no more, no less.

Teen Spirits uses the *dotted-eighth sixteenth* rhythm ⌐┐. Listen to the recording and play it the same way.

TEEN SPIRITS
Track 4

Chord changes is another word for chord progression. Try playing these power chord changes in the style of Nirvana's "Smells Like Teen Spirit."

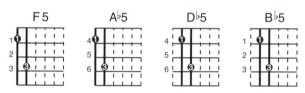

This sign ♭ is called a *flat*. When you see it next to a chord or note name, include "flat" in the name. For example A♭ is said "A flat." The flat is an *accidental*. Accidentals are musical symbols that tell us the pitch should be altered. A flat lowers a note one fret.

IRON LADY
Track 5

Now try these chord changes in the style of Black Sabbath's "Iron Man."

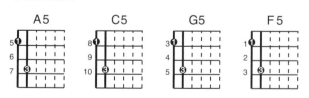

"Iron Lady" introduces *sixteenth notes*. A sixteenth note equals ¼ of a beat, so four sixteenths equal one beat.

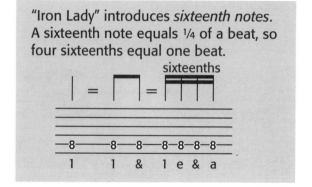

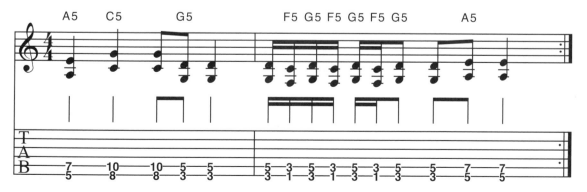

5 CHORDS — ANOTHER NAME FOR POWER CHORDS

- Power chords are also called *5 chords* because they consist of two notes that are five notes apart in the musical alphabet (which is A–B–C–D–E–F–G, it then repeats over and over).

- The bottom note is the *root*, which is the note that gives the chord its name.

- The top note is the *5th*.

In a C5 chord, the root is C, and the 5th is G (they are five notes apart: C=1, D=2, E=3, F=4, G=5). In an F5 chord, the root is F and the 5th is C.

The horizontal fretboard diagram below illustrates how we count up from the root, through the musical alphabet, to find a 5th. In this case, we count up from C on the 5th string and find a G on a higher fret. Then, to make our C5 chord, we play the same note G, but on the 4th string. You'll notice that we're skipping a fret between C and D, then D and E, but not between E and F. That's how the musical alphabet works on the guitar—never skip a fret from E to F, or from B to C.

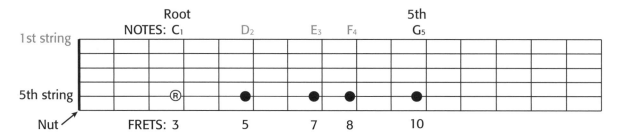

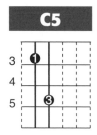

C5

If you're in a band with two guitarists, one of you can play power chords while the other plays the same chords as open or barre chords. This can create a bigger, broader sound for certain parts of your songs. You can also try this if your band has a guitarist and a keyboard player (letting the guitarist play the power chords.)

HOW TO LEARN THE POWER CHORD NAMES

How did I learn the power chord names? First I made sure I knew what the names of the notes were on the E and A strings. I started by memorizing the note names at the 3rd, 5th, 7th and 12th frets. When you have memorized those spots, filling in the blanks (1st and 2nd, 4th, 6th, 8th, 9th thru 11th) is pretty easy. Add the shape of the chord, water, stir, and voila... you're done.

Ann Klein, *guitarist, mandolin/dobro/lap steel player, singer, composer (Ani DiFranco, Joan Osborne, various Broadway shows, solo artist)*

Most power chords are moveable. At each fret position, the chord gets a different letter name. As explained on page 18, the musical alphabet is made up of seven letters: A, B, C, D, E, F, and G. So if you know where to find the note B on the 6th and 5th strings, you'll know at least two ways of playing a B5 chord.

Let's play the notes on the 6th and 5th strings all the way up to the 12th fret. Play each note with your index finger. Notice that all the notes are two frets apart except E–F and B–C. Those notes are only one fret apart.

Notes on the 5th and 6th Strings

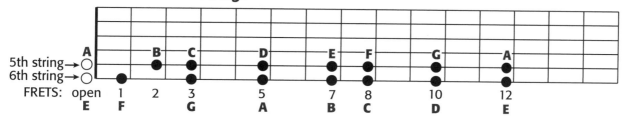

Which Notes Are Missing?

Here's the fretboard again. Can you fill in the names of the missing notes?

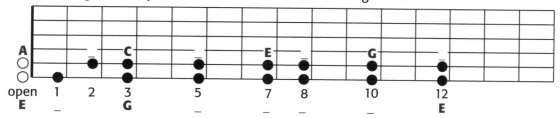

Here Are the Root Notes–Can You Play the Power Chords?

Here's a chord progression in the style of Green Day's "Oh Love." We've only written out the root notes of each chord. Can you play the power chords connected to each root note?

AA D AA DDDG AA

THE REPEAT SIGN

If you see a *repeat sign* at the end of an example or song—double dots on the inside of the thick-thin double bars—go back to the beginning and play it again!

ROCK, INDIE, AND BLUES RHYTHM PLAYING

CAN'T STAND MYSELF - I LOVE YOU

Track 6

Try some classic hard rock in the style of Joan Jett's "I Hate Myself for Loving You." Sometimes it sounds cool to let the last chord of a phrase taper off with a *slide*. It happens twice in this track. Listen to the E5 chord that comes right after the D5.

Here's how you do it: hit the E5 and keep your fingers pressed down against the strings as you slide them down just a fret or two in the direction of the headstock. That makes the chord sound like it's tapering off.

A *slide*, indcated with a line before or after a note in the TAB and music, is done by gliding the finger along the string without releasing pressure, creating a smooth, vocal, gliding sound. See page 58 for more.

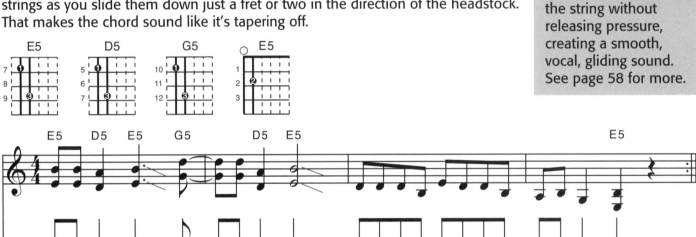

COURTNEY'S DOLLS

Track 7

Try this 1990s indie rock piece in the style of Hole's "Doll Parts." You'll get to play a three-bar figure. Count the beats in each bar ("one, two, three, four; two, two, three, four; three, two, three, four…") as you listen to the track. This will help you hear how long to hold the E5 chord, and know when to come back in.

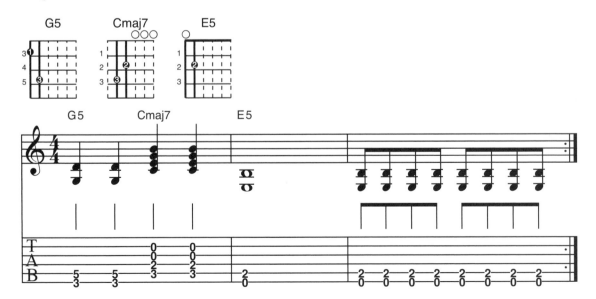

STINGIN' BEE BLUES

Here's a bluesier bit in the style of Memphis Minnie's "Bumble Bee." We'll cover more blues rhythm guitar and check out what guitarists like Ana Popovic, Sue Foley, Bonnie Raitt, and Deborah Coleman play in this genre in a later section.

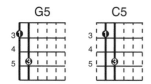

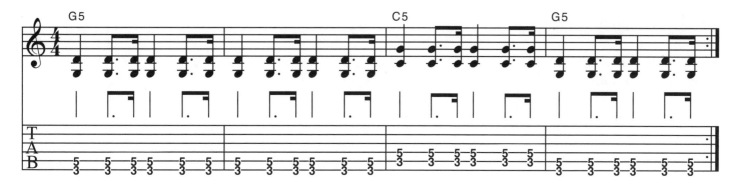

 Practice all the exercises with a *metronome*. That's a device that makes a steady clicking sound that you can make slower or faster. You can also find metronome apps online. Using a metronome will help develop your time-keeping skill (a *steady sense of the beat*).

Many musicians like metronomes that also have a blinking red light in addition to the click, so that they can see the beat as well as hear it.

PHOTO BY • Francis Schonken

Electronic metronome

"Learning different blues standards really makes learning power chord names easy, since they always have a I–IV–V chord progression. I first learned that progression from the 6th string downwards, and then I learned the same songs from the 5th string upwards."

Ana Popovic, blues guitarist, singer and songwriter

RIFFS WITH POWER CHORDS

Photo by Glen La Ferman

"A great rock riff must have a great tone, a memorable and anthem-like melody, and the perfect length and rhythm."

Kat Dyson, *guitarist, singer and composer (Prince, Cyndi Lauper, P-Funk Allstars)*

A *riff* is a short and catchy musical theme that repeats in a song. It can make a song instantly recognizable and pull people in, making them want to hear more.

 SMOKY WATERS

Track 9

Try playing this riff in the style of Deep Purple's "Smoke on the Water."

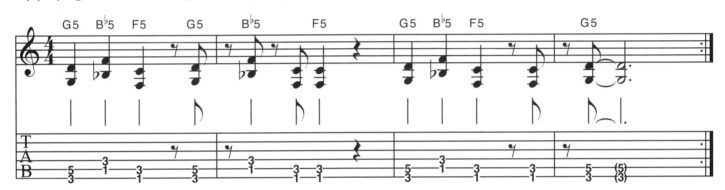

PLAYING POWER CHORDS WITH THREE STRINGS

You get three-string power chords by adding the octave of the root with your pinkie. An octave is eight note steps higher than the root in the major scale.

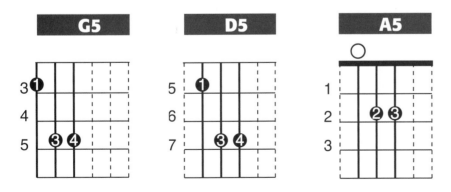

Still struggling to learn the names of those power chords? Completely understandable! Pick a three-chord song from a punk, blues, or folk songbook. Look at the first letter in each chord's name; find that note on the 6th or 5th string (page 21), and then play the matching power chord. For example: if a song includes the chords G, C, and D, play the power chords G5, C5, and D5.

* When notes are tied (see page 148), the fret number in parenthesis tells you not to pick that note again.

PALM MUTING

Palm muting is a guitar technique that creates a muffled, percussive sound. You hear it a lot in more aggressive rock styles (the "chugga-chugga" sound), but also in pop hits like Adele's "Rolling in the Deep." Palm-muted chords or single notes are great for creating different dynamics and textures within a song.

Here's how you do it:

Rest the heel of your right hand where the strings end, right by the bridge of your guitar. The heel is the cushy part of your palm, above the wrist, on the pinkie side. Let it touch the strings very lightly as you pick them.

The trick is not to press too hard or soft with your right hand, as this will make the notes sound either too quiet or too "normal." This takes some repeated practice.

Palm muting

PALM MUTING STRINGS

Track 10

Listen to the track. First, the D5 chord is played normally, and then palm-muted. Compare the difference. Now you try it! You can play it slower if it's hard.

In tablature, palm muting is often abbreviated as "P.M."

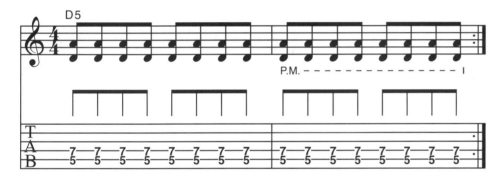

PALM MUTING, AMERICANA-ROCK STYLE: "SHE CANT WIND DOWN"

Track 11

Let's play palm muted chords in a rootsy, Americana-rock style, similar to Tom Petty's "I Won't Back Down."

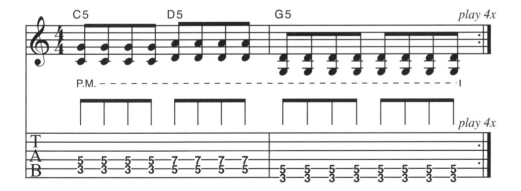

We skipped the chord diagrams for these exercises, since they've appeared in the book before. If you're unsure how to play these chords, go to page 21.

PALM MUTING EXERCISE—METAL AND PUNK-STYLE: "NEVER MORE"

Track 12

These are two fun but more challenging palm-muted riffs in the style of Metallica's
"Through the Never." You'll palm mute most of the power chords and the short melody
played on single notes. The track is played at 130bpm (beats per minute—you can use
your metronome). With practice, you can speed it up to 188bpm, like the original song.

Note: Please make sure you follow the left-hand fingering guideline below the TAB to
play the single-note melody correctly. It's very important.

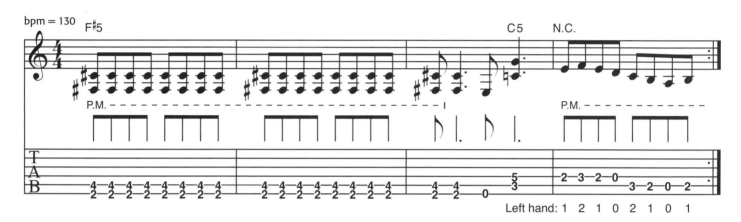

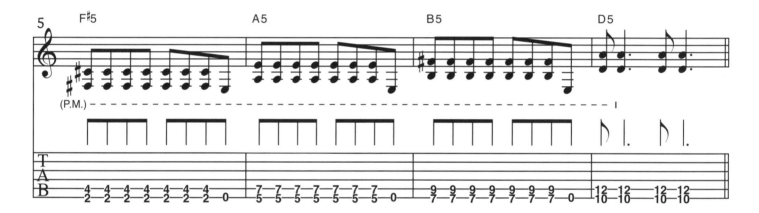

P.M.	= palm muting
N.C.	= no chord
Left hand 1	= index finger
Left hand 2	= middle finger

You can hear these kinds of guitar parts in metal, punk, and hardcore songs. You might
also notice that these rock styles use lots of distortion to create more aggressive guitar
sounds. You can learn more about amps, pedals, and effects such as distortion in
Section 5.

Your Creative Task Write your own power chord riff in TAB! Make it palm muted or not,
fast and furious or laid back…however you like. Just indicate the
strings and fret numbers you're playing—you don't need to worry
about the rhythmic notation. But you can add the repeat sign if
needed. And if your riff is palm muted, write a little "P.M." below the
riff (you'll see where it's located in the previous examples.)

Blues Rhythm Guitar: The Shuffle

Thousands of rock songs are based on the classic blues shuffle rhythm, so knowing how to play it is essential for a rock guitarist. Let's check it out.

 THE SHUFFLE SOUND
Track 13

Let's listen to one bar of notes played in groups of three followed by a bar of long-short rhythms. Hear the difference? This is called a *shuffle* rhythm.

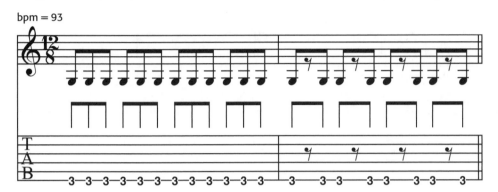

> A *shuffle* has a distinctive, bouncy feel. It's driven by a *triplet* rhythm (three eighth notes in the time of two). But in a shuffle triplet, the second eighth note is replaced by a rest, so that you only hear the first and third eighth notes of the triplet. This is what creates the "bounce."

 FIRST SHUFFLE EXERCISE: ROLLIN' DOWN THE BIG ROAD
Track 14

This rhythm ⌐. ⌐ is used to show the shuffle feel. You'll also find the word "Shuffle" at the beginning of the example. Let's play a shuffle similar to Sue Foley's "Down the Big Road Blues," but simplified. You'll play the A, D, and E power chords, with the root notes on the open 5th, 4th, and 6th strings for each respective chord. (Music readers: the notation for these exercises is one way of notating shuffle rhythms.)

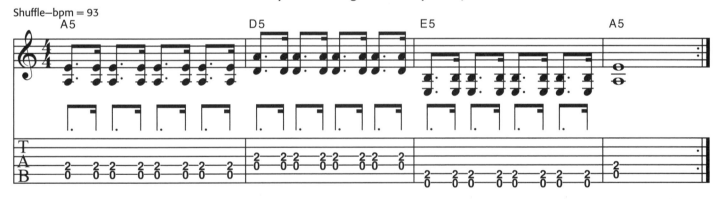

 CAN YOU SHAKE IT LIKE THAT?
Track 15

Now let's try a new shuffle pattern in the style of Ana Popovic's "How'd You Learn to Shake It Like That." You'll play the same chords, but add a new note with your ring finger on beats two and four.

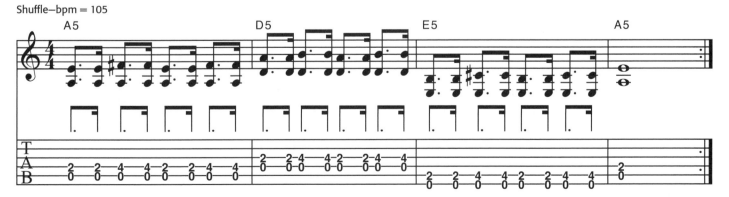

 **PLAY IT IN G**

Let's play the previous pattern with other chords. Hold down the main chord with your 1st and 3rd finger. Stretch your 4th finger to play the note on beats two and four!

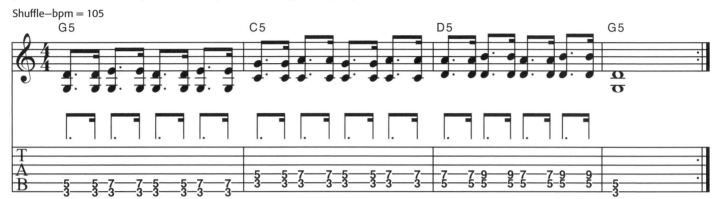

 LOVE ME LIKE YOU CAN (for more experienced players)

Track 17

This quintessential shuffle pattern is in the style of Bonnie Raitt's "Love Me Like a Man" and many other blues songs. Play the note on beat two with your 3rd finger, and the note on beat three with your 4th finger. Once you can play this easily in A as written, try doing it in G for a bigger stretch.

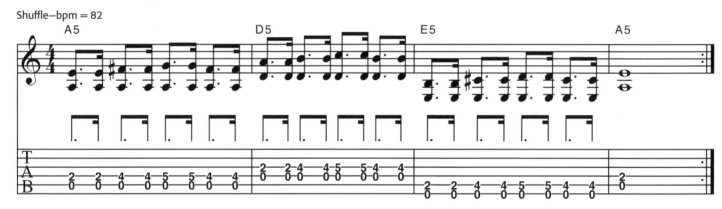

A faster rock variation (without the shuffle "bounce") can be heard on Foo Fighter's "The Pretender."

To learn more about playing blues, check out the section on I–IV–V chords (page 53), then move on to 12-bar blues (page 55.)

"A shuffle can be played with a lot of different feels: country, rock, Texas style, traditional blues, etc... But the most important thing to remember is: it has to swing.

Just because it's based on a simple structure does not mean it's easy to play. Playing blues challenges your musicality to develop the deeper aspects of your musicianship: good tone on your instrument, timing, phrasing, dynamics, texture, tension and release, expression and feel. If you work on these things, your playing in any style of music will grow exponentially."

Sue Foley, *guitarist, singer and songwriter (He Said, She Said, solo artist)*

Photo by Andrew MacNaughtan

CORRECT FINGERING MAKES ALL THE DIFFERENCE

You don't want to play all your riffs, melodies or solos with just your index finger or two fingers. Correct fingering helps you to find your way around the guitar. It allows you to hit the notes you intend to hit without having to look down at your guitar. It also frees you up to play busier or faster parts with ease and fluidity.

The Guiding Principle for Fingering

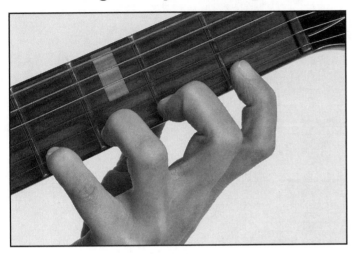

Let's say you're playing something that's within the first four frets of the guitar.

- Use your 1st finger to play any notes that are on the 1st fret.
- Use your 2nd finger to play any notes on the 2nd fret.
- Use your 3rd finger to play any notes on the 3rd fret.
- And yes, use your 4th finger to play any notes on the 4th fret (you can do it!)

What if you're playing something that's within the 2nd–5th fret, or higher? Apply the same principle: 1st finger for the first fret in the range, 2nd finger for the second fret in the range; 3rd finger for the third fret in the range, etc. (And this goes for any of the strings you're playing.)

 ## FINGERING EXERCISE: UP AND DOWN THE STAIRCASE
Track 18

This exercise will help you learn which fingers to use on which frets; it's great to do before a practice session, rehearsal, or show. Make sure you play the notes with your fingertips and use alternate picking. You can play it up and down the fretboard, and across all six strings. Since strings and frets vary in size, you'll get to know your guitar better and improve your hand's ability to stretch at lower, wider frets.

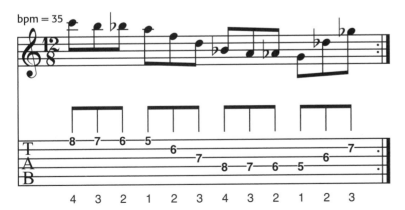

WALKING BASS LINES AND CHORD WALK-UPS

Adding a *walking bass* line between chords, or moving from one chord to another in gradual steps, is a great way of creating variety in your rhythm guitar playing. It can give a song a driving feel. Don't use these effects too much, however, in a single song—just here and there for extra "spice."

 YOU ROCK ME ALRIGHT

Track 19

Let's play a walking bass figure over an E5 chord in the style of what Susan Tedeschi plays in "Rock Me Right." Note: the rhythm is more of a straight rock rhythm and not a shuffle. Follow the left-hand fingering guideline below the TAB.

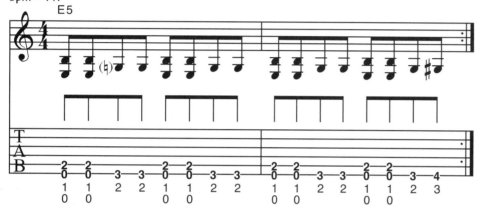

 HIGHER AND HIGHER

Track 20

Let's get familiar with this classic walk-up riff, where power chords move higher and higher from the A5 up to the D5 chord to build more intensity in the transition. You'll hear this kind of ascending walk-up line in Led Zeppelin's "Rock and Roll" and in many blues songs.

 The bluesy rhythm guitar phrases that you've learned mostly revolved around the A chord. Once you're comfortable playing them, make sure to try them out with other power chords like G, C, D, E, B, and F.

How do you do this? Go back to page 28 and revisit the exercise "Play It in G" (Track 16). See how the first power chord starts at the 6th string, 3rd fret? That's where the note G is located, so the chord is a G5 chord.

If you want to play an example in C instead of A, find the C5 chord that starts at the 5th string, 3rd fret, and play all your blues rhythm guitar phrases from there.

ACCENTED RHYTHMS

A great way to make your rhythm guitar parts catchier is to accent some of the notes by picking them a little harder than the others. You can hear this in many indie rock songs, like Kings of Leon's "Use Somebody."

In these examples you'll play just a G5 chord for now. Play downstrokes with the pick the entire time. Any notes that have the accent sign above them, you want to pick a little harder, so that they pop out more than the other notes.

Below is the standard symbol for an *accent*. It appears above or below the note to be accented.

 ### I COULD USE SOMEONE
Track 21

This example is in the style of Kings of Leon's "Use Somebody", but half as fast.

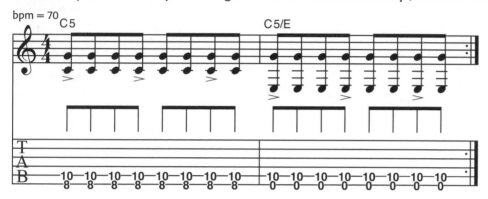

 ### I NEED ANOTHER HOUR
Track 22

This example resembles the rhythm of Sleater-Kinney's "One More Hour" (at 141 bpm) and Grace Potter & The Nocturnals' "Money" (at 110 bpm.)

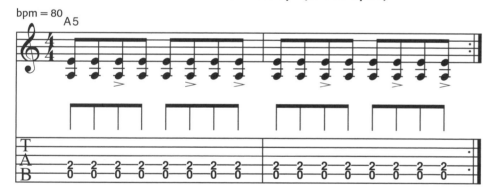

 ### A PLANT, RAG, AND A BAG
Track 23

This example is in the style of PJ Harvey's "Plants and Rags." The first bar resembles a drummer hitting the snare drum on beats 2 and 4 in a typical rock beat.

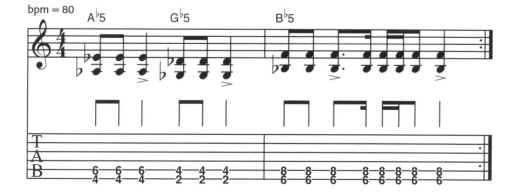

PUTTING IT ALL TOGETHER

Congratulations! You made it through the power chord section of the book! Put what you've learned to use and play a longer song, "She Wrote on the Ceiling." This one is in the style of The Black Key's "Gold on the Ceiling."

The song has three sections. Note the repeat signs at the end of sections two (bars 4–7) and three (bars 8–12). When you encounter a left-facing repeat :‖ within a song, go back to the right-facing repeat ‖: you passed on the way there.

On the CD, there's a *fuzz* (distortion) effect on the guitar, but you don't need to get that.

You'll play a palm-muted intro riff, power chords, a step-wise walk-up, and another riff with accented notes—all with a shuffle feel. Follow the left-hand fingering guidelines for all the single-note sections; you'll find these below the TAB. Have fun!

> This sign ♯ is called a *sharp*. When you see it next to a chord or note name, include "sharp" in the name. For example F♯ is said "F sharp." Like the flat, a sharp is an accidental. It raises a note by one fret.

Chords Used

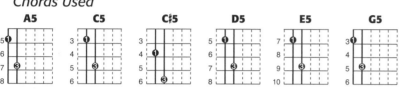

SHE WROTE ON THE CEILING

Track 24

Shuffle—bpm = 130

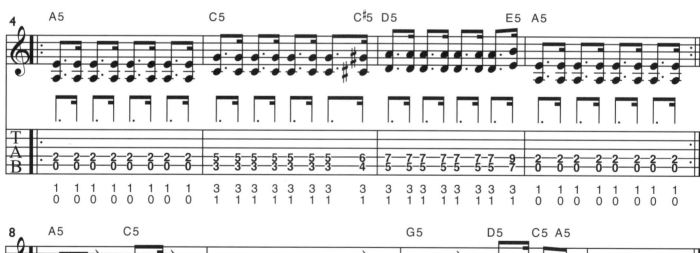

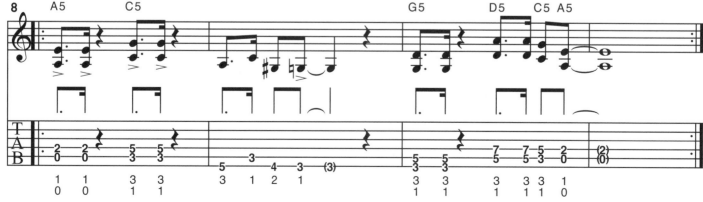

Open-Chord Playing in Rock

Open chords aren't only used in "campfire songs" and acoustic music. They're played in rock as well. Sometimes guitarists play them in certain spots of a song just to achieve a sonic effect—the big sound of open strings, for instance. Open chords are called "open" because they include one or more open strings.

These combinations of open chords are great for you to know as a rock guitarist.

FIRST OPEN CHORDS

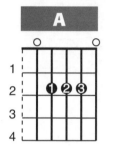
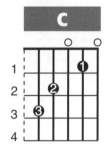
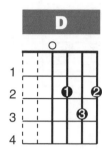
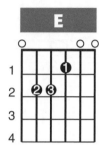
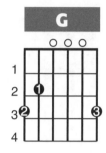

 DIRTY CHEAP DEEDS

Track 25

This open chord riff is in the style of AC/DC's "Dirty Deeds Done Dirt Cheap."

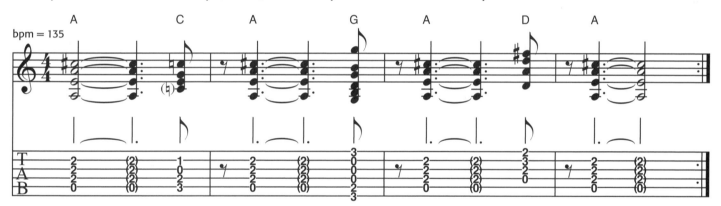

 MY SWEET CHILD

Track 26

Try playing this chord progression, which is in the style of Guns N' Roses' "Sweet Child O' Mine." Follow the right-hand picking guideline under the chord symbols at the top.

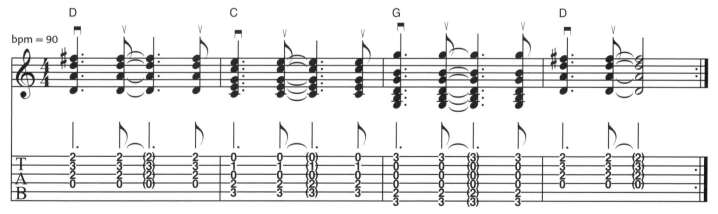

Chords Used

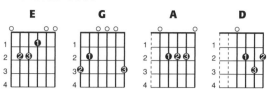

HOW MANY TIMES

Track 27

This chord riff in E is in the style of Led Zeppelin's "How Many More Times."

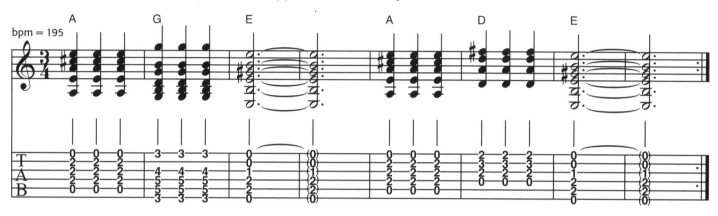

FIRST MINOR CHORD

All the open chords you have played so far are *major* chords, which have a happy or even heroic sound. Now you'll learn your first *minor* chord. Compared to major chords, minor chords sound sad, or serious. Chords that just have a letter name are major. For example, "E" is E Major. Minor chords will have an "m" after the letter. For example "Em" is E Minor. Try comparing the sounds of E Major and E Minor to understand the difference in sound. By the way, power chords are neither major nor minor.

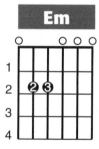

DANCING WITH HER BARE FEET

Track 28

Try these chord changes, which are inspired by Patti Smith's "Dancing Barefoot." The root notes of the Em and D chords at the end are palm muted.

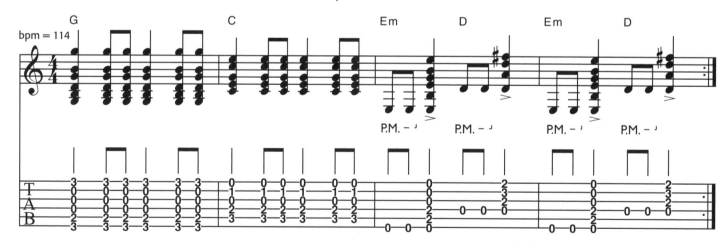

If the chord changes in these exercises are difficult for you, then by all means practice them slower. Also, note that playing these rhythms slow, medium or fast will result in very different feels, so experiment with the *tempos* (speeds) and see what you like.

PICKING ARPEGGIOS

Have you heard the Metallica ballad "Nothing Else Matters"? The intro to that song shows how you can play a chord by picking one note at a time, instead of strumming all the notes at once. A chord that's played this way is called an *arpeggio* ("broken chord").

The technique of using your right-hand fingers to pick each note is called *fingerpicking*. We're going to use the guitar pick, instead. Follow the picking guidelines below the TAB.

 BROKEN E MINOR

Track 29

Here's an exercise to introduce you to picking arpeggios. We'll use an Em chord.

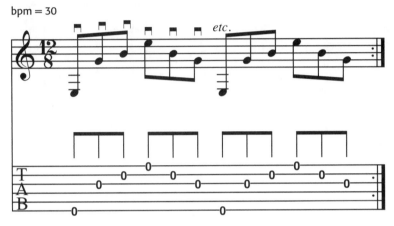

I've got an acoustic guitar picking tip: use a large triangle pick that's very light for that shimmery sound...

Kat Dyson, *guitarist, singer and composer (Prince, Cyndi Lauper, P-Funk Allstars)*

 MINOR CHIMES

Track 30

Now we're going to try a different picking pattern for the same Em chord. Position your left hand into the Em chord shape before you begin.

HOTEL LAUREL CANYON

Track 31

This is a much more complex pattern in the style of the Eagles' "Hotel California." It uses notes from the Am and E chords. Note the use of accents.

Am

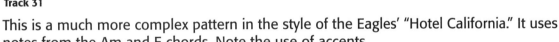
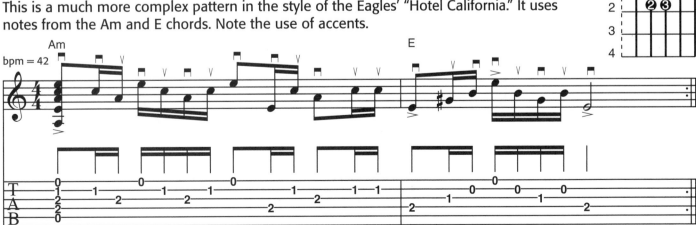

Practice the arpeggios on page 35 slowly and make sure all the notes ring out clearly. Try them with different chords, and make up your own patterns. Mixing arpeggios and strummed chords can make your songs more interesting.

BASS-CHORD STRUMS, WALKING BASS, AND DRONE CHORDS

Bass-Chord Strums

Bass-chord strumming is a cool playing style rooted in country and bluegrass and originally used by players like Mother Maybelle Carter. It's been adapted by many rock artists and we're going to try a strum like this, rock-style. We hit a clear bass note on the first beat, and then play a full chord on the second beat.

In this strumming style, we often use extra notes between the main chords to create the sound of a moving bass line. This creates a new type of chord called a *slash chord*. To the left of the slash is the chord name, to the right of the slash is the name of the bass note. Familiarize yourself with the slash chords on the right.

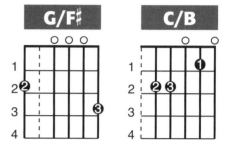

 ROCK 'N' ROLL EFFIGY

Track 32

Let's try this bass-chord strum, which is in the style of Gov't Mule's cover of "Effigy."

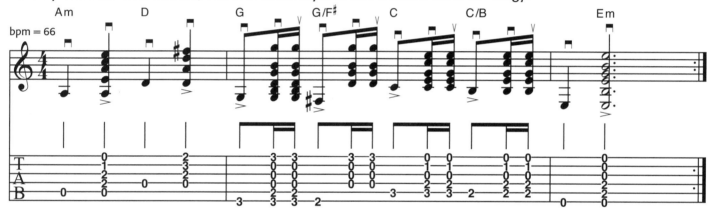

WALKING BASS

In the last exercise, you happened to play two walking bass lines in the second bar: the G bass note in the G chord moved down one fret to F♯, and the C bass note in the C chord moved down one fret to B. Walking bass lines can really build a song and make the listener anticipate the chord changes more.

 IF ONLY YOU WERE HERE

Track 33

Try playing these chords with walking bass lines in the style of Pink Floyd's "Wish You Were Here." We'll "walk" from G to Em, then to A, and finally wrap it up in G.

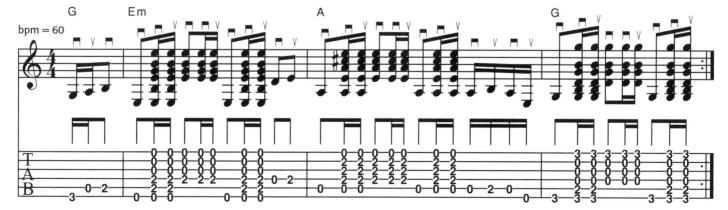

"The electric guitar has more mid-range sound than an acoustic, so it's really built to be part of an ensemble or provide accompaniment. There are notable and wonderful exceptions to this, but electric guitar isn't something you often hear completely solo for an extended length of time.

For the most part, I use electric when I have low frequencies like bass drums and highs like strings and percussion. A well built acoustic guitar is often just dying to be left alone, as it will have a huge range of audible frequencies and a lot more options when it comes to how you can put them to use.

Acoustics also have a much shorter natural decay than electrics, so you can hear the timing of that decay and use it for wonderful suspensions and dissonances that only last for a brief period.

I also use electric guitar and volume pedal for my own kind of 'synth' pads, because the volume pedal takes away the attack, and the lengthy decay of an electric makes it sound like you're holding down the keys on a synth."

Kaki King, *guitarist and composer*

DRONES AND SLASH CHORDS

The sound of *droning* open strings underneath a set of changing chords is one of the most beautiful sonic treats a guitarist can achieve. Drones—also called *pedal tones*—can create very colorful and exotic sounds from the use of *slash chords*, where a note other than the root, and maybe even from outside the chord, is played on the bottom. The bottom note is written to the right of the slash. For example, F/E is an F chord with an E in the bass. In the example below, the two top strings from E chord are also included in the F/E. Pete Townshend of The Who and Jimmy Page of Led Zeppelin often use drone chords in songs.

 SPANISH WINE

Track 34

Here's a little instant flamenco flavor you can get by simply moving an open E chord up one fret. Make sure you include the open 6th string (E) in both chords.

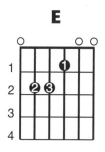

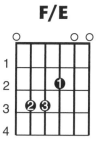

 ACROSS THE HILLS AND GONE

Track 35

The easiest way to create a drone chord is to pick a regular open chord, like D and move that shape up the neck and see what it sounds like at different fret positions. Play the open 4th string (D) with all the chords, like a drone. You can hear this concept at work in Led Zeppelin's "Over the Hills and Far Away."

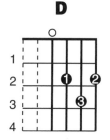 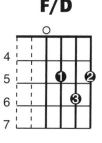 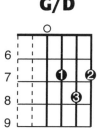 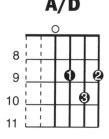

NOTE: As you move the D chord up the neck, it won't be called D anymore. For now, if you discover an interesting chord, don't worry about figuring out its name. Just draw a chord diagram of it and jot down the fingerings and fret position, so that you don't forget it!

PUTTING IT ALL TOGETHER

And now you've made it through the open chord section, too! Our "wrap-up" song this time is in the style of Led Zeppelin's "The Song Remains The Same."

You'll get to play drone chords with a rhythmically accented pedal tone, picked arpeggios, open chords with a walking bass line, and three-string power chords. Pay attention to the chords shown below; there are some new ones in the mix.

Chords Used

YOU WON'T REMAIN THE SAME

Track 36

Once you've played the walking bass in bar 7, stop the 6th string with the heel of your right hand so it isn't ringing when you strum the D chord.

Barre Chords

With barre chords, you lay your left index finger across five or six strings, and then shape the rest of the chord with your other left-hand fingers. They take some effort to learn at first, but along with power chords, they're the most common way of playing chords in rock, so let's dig in!

Typical barre chord

MAKING THE TRANSITION TO BARRE CHORDS

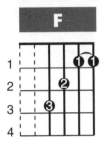

If barre chords are totally new to you, the best transition into them is by learning to play the basic four-string F chord. Here, you only have to do a "half barre" by laying your index finger across the 1st and 2nd strings, and then adding your 2nd and 3rd fingers to get the rest of the chord (see the photo above).

Learning F in Three Steps

If a four-string F feels too difficult to play, here's how you conquer it through three gradual steps.

1. Play a two-string version of the F chord, where you barre the 1st and 2nd strings at the 1st fret with your 1st finger.

2. Once you're comfortable playing that, add your 2nd finger to the 3rd string, 2nd fret.

3. Once that feels easy, move on to the final step: add your 3rd finger to the 4th string, 3rd fret.

NOTE: Remember not to play the strings that are shown as dotted lines.

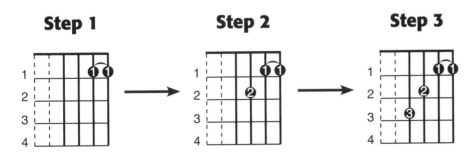

The main thing with barre chords is even finger pressure. What I mean by that is to distribute even pressure for all the strings involved to get a clean, full chord.

***Kat Dyson**, guitarist, singer and composer (Prince, Cyndi Lauper, P-Funk Allstars)*

Let's play an open chord progression in the *key of C**, where chances are very likely that you'll find an F chord. The feel of this one is in the style of Bob Marley's "No Woman No Cry."

Chords Used

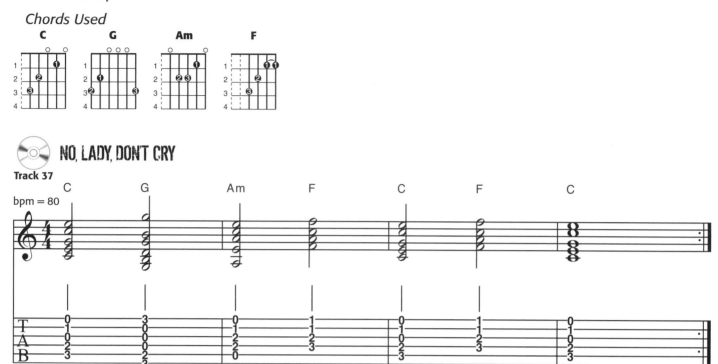

NO, LADY, DON'T CRY
Track 37

Try to learn and play as many songs that feature the F chord as you can, so that you get plenty of opportunities to practice the chord.

Exercise to Make Your Barre Finger Stronger

Here's a great exercise that you want to go through once a day until you can barre your finger across all six strings. Pick every string individually and make sure they all sound clear as little bells!

Press your left index finger down against the 1st string, 1st fret. Strike the note with your pick. If it sounds clean, press your finger against the 1st and 2nd strings at the same time. Pick the two notes separately, making sure they both ring clearly.

If they both sound clean, press your 1 finger against the 3rd string, as well. At this point, press the strings down with the left side of your finger. Pick the three notes separately.

If they sound clean, progressively add on one more string at a time until your 1st finger firmly is pressed down across all six strings, and they all ring clearly.

Track 38

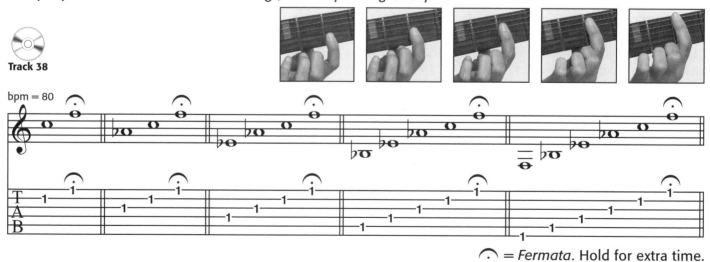

⌢• = *Fermata*. Hold for extra time.

* *Key* refers to the tonal center of a song. If the song starts and ends on C, and often returns to C at the ends of musical ideas, it is probably "in the key of C." It is a good idea to study music theory and gain a good grasp of this and similar musical concepts.

WHY LEARN BARRE CHORDS IF I KNOW POWER CHORDS AND OPEN CHORDS?

There are several good reasons:

1. Playing only power chords all the time ends up sounding a little one-dimensional. You need other types of chords to bring out contrast.

2. With barre chords, you get a broader tonal range similar to open chords, but without the ringing open strings. They are ideal for very rhythmic strums.

3. Many chord progressions are easier to play with barre chords than with open chords, especially if you're playing in sharp or flat keys (more on that soon).

Photo by Rebecca Wilson

"I was little, my hands were little—barre chords were torture! I remember feeling like a real guitar player as soon as I could fret a barre chord and not have it buzz. The only way to master them is to play them, and then play them some more."

Vicki Peterson, *guitarist, singer, songwriter (The Bangles, Continental Drifters)*

"You absolutely have to know barre chords because of these elements: reach, strength, dexterity. It tackles a lot at once! It is the building block for so many elements of playing guitar, for example, playing a major seventh chord, which looks similar in shape to the major barre chord. It is also the building block for just about every rock guitar song. You can't get away with not knowing it. It's a physical and audible necessity!"

Ann Klein, *guitarist, mandolin/dobro/lap steel player, singer, composer (Ani DiFranco, Joan Osborne, various Broadway shows, solo artist).*

If you are a total newbie on guitar, you can substitute power chords or open chords for the barre chords in this section (when possible). Once you're comfortable playing open chords, power chords, and the blues riffs, try the four-string F chord and then move on to learning barre chords.

E-SHAPED BARRE CHORDS

E-shaped barre

The E Shapes

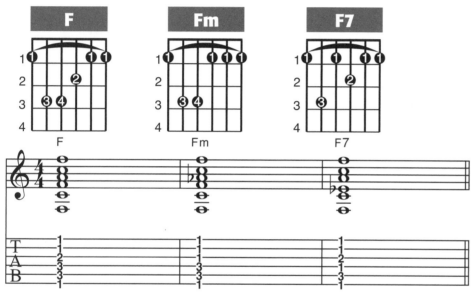

Just as with power chords, you can move barre chords up and down the neck.

Notice in the chord diagrams how the barre chord shapes look very similar to the open E chords at the top of the page. Your 1st finger will lay across the strings, while your 2nd, 3rd, and 4th fingers will form shapes that look like the open E chords.

Track 39

Practice E-Shaped Barre Chords

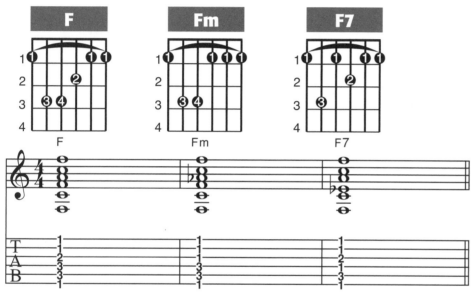

These chords have their root note on the 6th string (low E.) The major chords are based on the open E major chord shape; the minor chords on the E minor chord shape, and the bluesy *dominant 7th** chords are based on the open E7 chord shape.

Track 40

LADDER TO THE CLOUDS

Here's a rock chord progression in the style of Led Zeppelin's "Stairway to Heaven" that uses only E-shape barre chords.

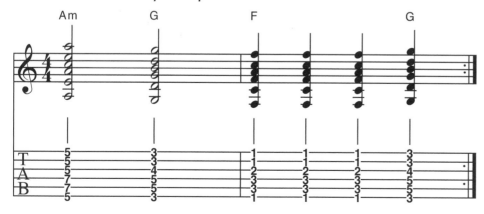

* The dominant 7th chord is a chord based on the fifth chord in a key. For example, if a song is in C, the fifth chord in the key is G (C_1, D_2, E_3, F_4, G_5). It's a 7th chord, which means it has a note that is seven notes higher than its root. The root is G, so the 7th is F (G_1, A_2, B_3, C_4, D_5, E_6, F_7).

SILENCE AND RESTS

As you have already seen, just as there are signs for playing pitches and rhythms in music, there also are signs for indicating *not* to play. These moments of silence are called *rests*.

If you want a quick silencing effect, you can stop the sound of your strings by lightly touching them with the heel of your strumming hand.

 Quarter Rest

This sign indicates silence for one count.

Half Rest

This sign indicates silence for two counts.

Whole Rest

This sign indicates silence for a whole bar. That means four counts if you're playing in $\frac{4}{4}$ time, three counts if you're playing in $\frac{3}{4}$ time, etc.

Practice Rests

Try playing these three E-shaped barre chords. The first two chords are each followed by a quarter rest. Hold the third chord for two beats, then follow it with a half rest. Mute the strings with a light touch of your right hand during each rest.

Track 41

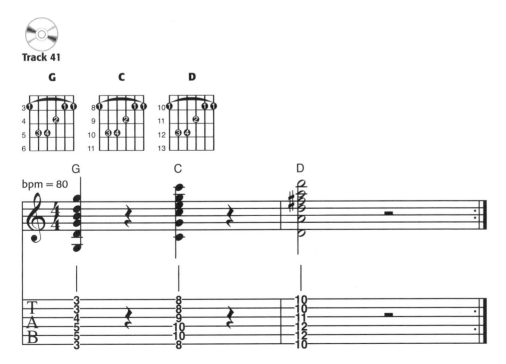

A-SHAPED BARRE CHORDS

Track 42

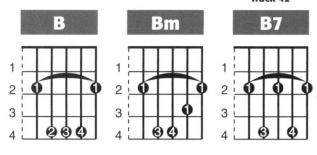

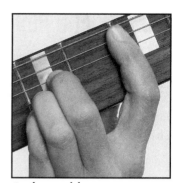

A-shaped barre.

These chords have their roots on the 5th string (A). The major chords are based on the open A major chord shape; the minor chords on the A minor chord shape, and the dominant seventh chords are based on the open A7 chord shape.

SHE'S WATCHING FROM THE TOWER

Track 43

Here's a chord progression in the style of Jimi Hendrix's version of Bob Dylan's "All Along the Watchtower" using A-shaped barre chords and quarter rests.

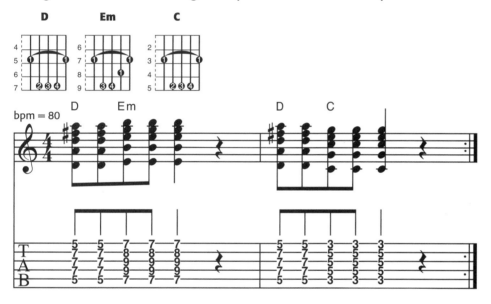

BARRICADE

Track 44

This riff is in the style of Heart's "Barracuda." The gallop rhythm of the palm-muted A5 chord sounds like "one, and-a-two, and-a-three, and-a-four, and-a." Listening to the CD will make it easy for you to learn.

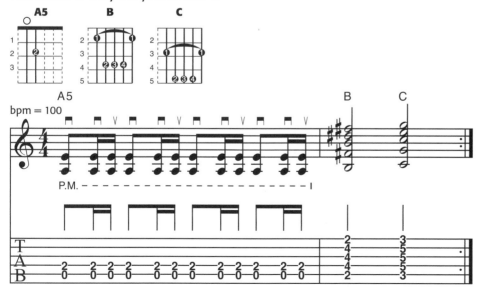

SHARPS AND FLATS

You were briefly introduced to the flat and sharp signs earlier in this book (pages 19 and 32, respectively). Let's take a closer look at accidentals.

The musical alphabet is made up of seven letters: A–B–C–D–E–F–G. The notes that are named after these seven letters are called the *natural notes*.

There are also notes between most of the naturals. They're commonly referred to as accidentals, and are either sharps or flats. The sharp sign (♯) raises the note a half step, while the flat sign (♭) lowers it a half step. The D on the 3rd fret of the 2nd string can be lowered to become D♭. The C on the 1st fret of that string can be raised to become C♯. This is an example of how an accidental can be called by either a flat name, or a sharp name. Two notes that sound the same but have different names are said to be *enharmonically* related.

SHARPS AND FLATS ON THE GUITAR

Take a look at your guitar fretboard, and focus on the 5th and 6th strings. Let's locate the natural notes and the sharp/flat notes on each of those strings.

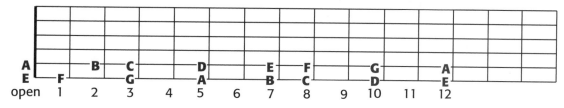

Look at the natural notes F and G on the 6th string at the 1st and 3rd frets. The note at the 2nd fret can be called either F♯ or G♭. Look at the frets between other natural notes and think about their sharp and flat names. Notice, also, that the note at the 12th fret is the same as the name of the open string. On all six strings of the guitar, the musical alphabet starts all over again at the 12th fret.

WHOLE STEPS AND HALF STEPS ON THE GUITAR

Notice how some notes are two frets apart, while others are right next to each other. In the guitar world, we call the distance of two frets a *whole step*, and the distance of one fret a *half step*.

Now look at the notes B to C, and E to F. These notes are only one fret apart on the guitar. There is a half step between B and C, and between E and F.

Instead of calling a note "B-sharp," we usually call it C. Instead of "E-sharp," it's usually F. Instead of "C-flat," we say "B;" instead of "F-flat" we say "E."

Exercise No. 1

Draw the natural notes of the 6th string with a black pen. With a blue pen, draw the notes G♭ and B♭.

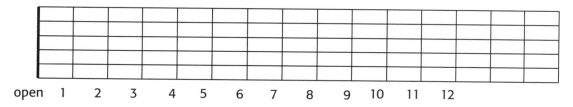

Exercise No. 2

Draw the natural notes of the 5th string with a black pen. With a blue pen, draw the notes C♯ and G♯.

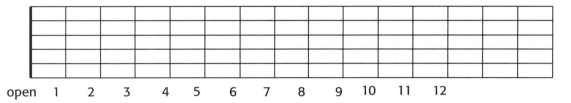

open 1 2 3 4 5 6 7 8 9 10 11 12

You can check your work by turning the book upside down and checking the diagram on the right:

STOKE MY FIRE

Track 45

Let's try this chord progression in the style of The Doors' "Light My Fire."

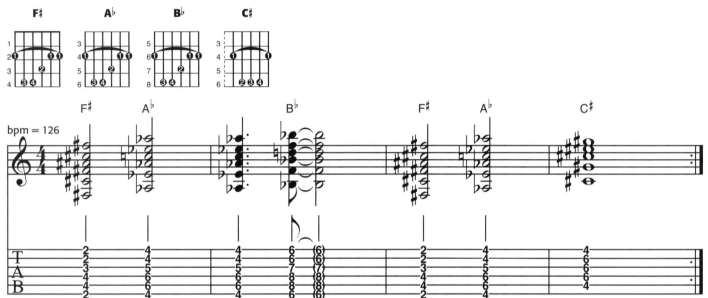

HE WON'T SPEAK

Track 46

Now try playing this chord progression in the style of No Doubt's "Don't Speak."

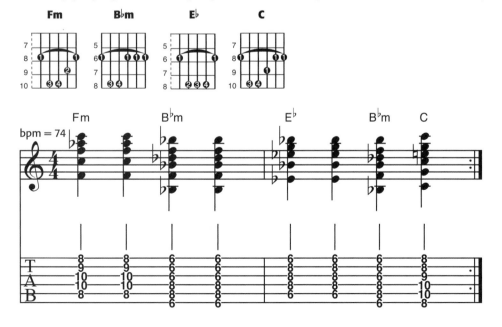

EXERCISE FOR MEMORIZING BARRE CHORDS

Playing songs is the best way to learn where to play all the barre chords. But following is an exercise that will also help.

Play just major chords the first time, then play the exercise with just minor chords. The third time around, only play dominant 7th chords. Play four strums per chord.

Remember that you can play a C barre chord in two different ways—with an A-shaped chord starting at the 3rd fret of the 5th string, or an E-shaped chord at the 8th fret of the 6th string. All other barre chords can be played with either an E-shaped or an A-shaped chord.

When you move from one chord to another, play the shapes that are closest to each other. For example, both the C and G chords can be played at the 3rd fret.

Keep in mind:

$G^\flat$ is located in the same place as $F^\sharp$. In other words, $G^\flat = F^\sharp$.

$D^\flat = C^\sharp$

$A^\flat = G^\sharp$

$E^\flat = D^\sharp$

$B^\flat = A^\sharp$

Next, we'll be going over some great strumming patterns in rock. It'll be fun! Once you've learned some of the strums, come back to this barre chord exercise. Try to play through all the chords in it, using the same strum pattern.

"They [barre chords] were really hard initially to play, because you have to build up strength. There is no quick way really... just spending a lot of time practicing."

Orianthi Panagaris, *guitarist, singer and songwriter (Michael Jackson, Alice Cooper, solo artist)*

ROCK STRUMMING

As a rhythm guitarist, you have a lot of power. If you play a great rhythm part with lots of feel, you can make a singer or soloist sound amazing. You contribute greatly to the feel of the song not only through the chords you choose to play, but also with the rhythms in which you choose to play them.

A Quick Review on Strumming Notation Before We Start

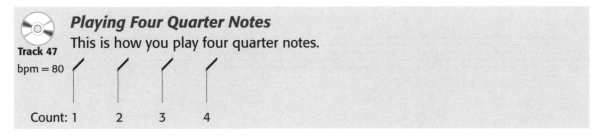

This is called a quarter note. It equals one beat.

Count: 1

Playing Four Quarter Notes
Track 47

This is how you play four quarter notes.

bpm = 80

Count: 1   2   3   4

Playing Eighth Notes
Track 48

These are two eighth notes connected by a beam. Together, they equal one beat. Let's play them.

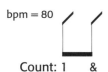

bpm = 80

Count: 1   &

Playing Four Beats of Eighth Notes
Track 49

Here are four beats of music played in eighth notes.

bpm = 80

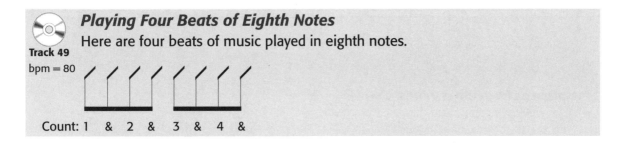

Count: 1 & 2 & 3 & 4 &

Playing Four Sixteenth Notes
Track 50

These are four sixteenth notes connected by double beams. Together, they equal one beat. Let's play them.

bpm = 80

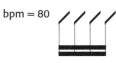

Count: 1 e & a

The Rests (Moments of Silence)

This is called a quarter rest. It equals one beat.

This is called an eighth rest. It equals half of one beat.

MUST-KNOW STRUM PATTERNS IN ROCK

Let's play some very useful strum patterns for rock and related styles like pop, reggae, ska, country-rock, punk, indie, folk and blues that you hear today.

Listen to the CD to hear what each example sounds like. Once you play them, follow the picking pattern of up or down strokes exactly as shown in each example. Tempos are indicated for each strum, so practice with a metronome.

How to Practice the Strums

If it's too hard for you to change chords and keep up a strum, start playing the example with one chord, then try two or three chords. Slow down your metronome, so you can change chords without pausing between each one.

Track 51

Rock or R&B with Hits on Beats 2 and 4

This is a rhythm you need to play with barre chords to get the right "snap."

bpm = 120

Track 52

Changing Chords on an Off-Beat

Changing chords just before the next bar begins creates a different feel, and it's a very common thing to do. So try changing chords on the "and" of beat 4.

bpm = 100

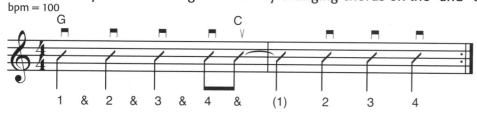

Track 53

Driving Eighth Notes with Accents on Beats 2 and 4

bpm = 114

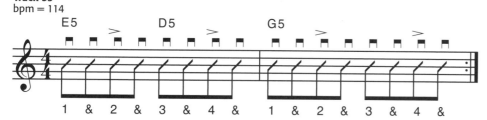

Track 54

Palm-Muted Barre Chords with Off-Beat

bpm = 100

Accents

Silence each chord after hitting it by muting the strings with your right hand. This will give the chord a good short "snap" sound, and prevent ringing strings.

On the tied notes in tracks 55–56, your picking hand comes down without touching the strings, then you touch the strings when you bring the pick back up. It's crucial to follow the picking to play these strums right!

Strum with One Tied Note

Track 55
bpm = 80

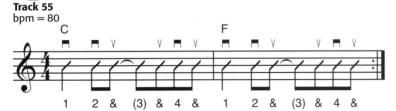

Strum with Two Tied Notes

Track 56 Once you can play this and the previous strum as written, here's a new challenge: try changing chords on the tied note! C and Am are two good chords for this.

bpm = 80

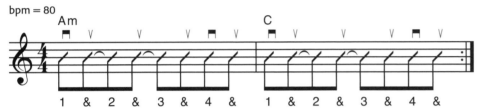

Fast Rock Groove with Chords on Beats 1 and 3

Track 57

bpm = 130

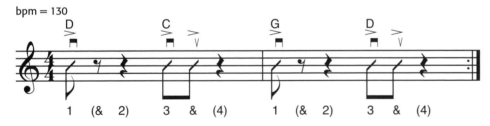

In the following muted strums, you'll silence strings with your left hand. Mute the chords by releasing the pressure of your left-hand fingers against the strings while still touching them, but not pressing them against the fretboard.

Classic Folk and Rock Strum

Track 58 The muted notes are marked with an "x."

bpm = 110

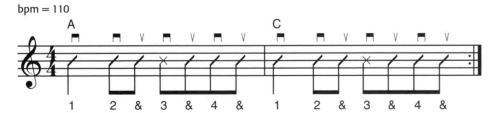

Driving Groove in the Style of "Proud Mary"

Track 59

bpm = 100

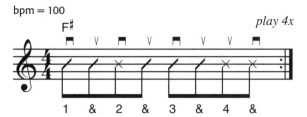

Basic Reggae Rhythms that Rockers Need to Know

Track 60

In Reggae and Ska circles, these guitar rhythms are often called "skank rhythms." They are great for punk and new wave rock, too. You can also hear them in Paul McCartney's "Live and Let Die" (and Guns N' Roses' cover of it). Let's try two variations of the "skank."

bpm = 70

 Quick Tip

When you use barre chords to play reggae or ska, you want to get out of the way of the bass guitar, so make your chords sound bright. Hold down the whole chord, but strum just the top three or four strings to get the right sound.

 Your Creative Task

Make up your own strum patterns! Mix and match parts of the different strums you've just learned. You can revisit examples from earlier in the book to get more ideas. Also, play the exercise on page 47 to practice both your strums and changing barre chords. You might get song ideas out of this…

"I love to play drums, so I'm always thinking about the beat and locking in… When working with Michael Jackson or Alice Cooper, there are a lot of rhythm parts when I'm not soloing away… and it's very important to pay attention to making them solid."

Orianthi Panagaris, *guitarist, singer and songwriter (Michael Jackson, Alice Cooper, solo artist)*

Photo: Facebook.com/shootingstarsmaui

PUTTING IT ALL TOGETHER

 CHAINS

Track 61

If you were totally new to barre chords, it probably took you a couple of weeks or months of dedicated practicing to get through this section. Great job!

In this song, inspired by David Bowie's "Changes," you'll play major, minor, and dominant 7th barre chords. In measure 9, you'll get to play open chords with walking bass lines, and then go back to barre chords for the last part at measure 13. If you want to, go back to the top and play it all over again.

Double bars show the end of a section.

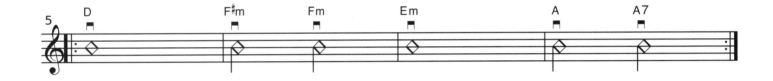

 Just listen to the track at first. Then follow the chord diagrams, slowly walking yourself through each chord, without playing any strumming patterns. As a final step, practice playing the chords with the right strums, but in a much slower tempo. Little by little, build up to the right speed.

Have fun. Hopefully this inspires you to write songs of your own. That's one of the important points of these exercises, besides building your guitar skills!

I-IV-V Chords — The Secret to Learning Lots of Songs

"Knowledge of common chord changes is a must at this level. When coming up with transitions or just communicating with a keyboardist or bass player, it's just as important to know the more intricate chords too. The m9, maj7ths, augmented, diminished, suspended, etc. are used quite a lot for a gig like Beyoncé."

Bibi McGill, *guitarist and musical director (Beyoncé, Pink, Paulina Rubio)*

Photo by Robin Harper

There are thousands of three-chord songs in almost every style of popular music. Often, these three chords form a progression that musicians refer to as I–IV–V (pronounced "one–four–five"). When you learn to recognize I–IV–V chord changes in songs, you'll be able to figure out lots of songs by ear easily and memorize them faster.

Roman Numerals							
I	II	III	IV	V	VI	VII	VIII
1	2	3	4	5	6	7	8

WHAT EFFECT DOES A I–IV–V HAVE IN A SONG?

- The I chord is the central chord of the song. Everything builds and resolves from it and toward it. Usually, the I chord starts off the song. It can often be the first or the last chord of the chorus. It is usually the very last chord of a song.

- The IV chord functions to build up the intensity and drive the song forward, but not as strongly as the V chord. The IV chord often resolves to the I chord. Some songs will end on the IV chord to create a mysterious, unresolved feeling.

- The V chord has the most drive and intensity. It often brings the song to a climactic point, such as the title line of a song, or right before a chorus begins.

COUNTING FOUR AND FIVE LETTERS FROM THE I CHORD

The IV and V chords are four and five note letters away from the I chord. Use the notes of the musical alphabet (page 18) to count forward. For example, in C, the I, IV and V chords will be C, F, and G (C_1 D_2 E_3 F_4 G_5). If the song is in D, the I–IV–V chords will be D–G–A (D_1 E_2 F_3 G_4 A_5).

In the beginning, it's easiest to practice counting I–IV–V chords in the keys C, G, D, A or E (in the other seven keys, there will be some sharp or flat chords).

EMMA IS A GUITAR SHREDDER (IN A)

Track 62

Let's play a I–IV–V progression in A in the style of The Ramones' "Sheena Is a Punk Rocker." The chords will be A5–D5–E5. Hear how each chord builds in intensity.

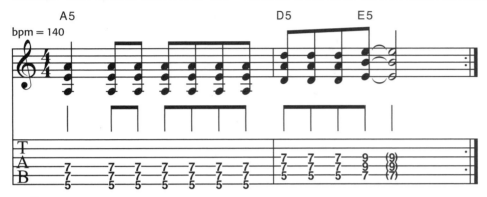

 ## GLASSES IN MY POCKET (IN G)

Track 63

Try playing this song in G, which is in the style of The Pretenders' "Brass In Pocket." This time the I–IV–V chords, G, C, and D, take up one song section each—verse, pre-chorus, and chorus—so that you can really hear the sonic effect of each chord and how it moves each section forward throughout the song.

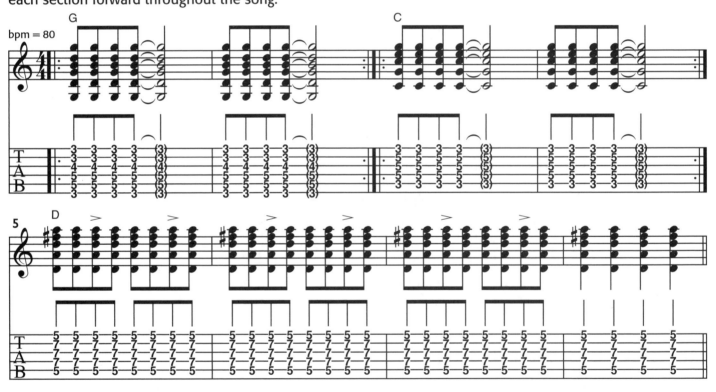

A TERM USED IN SONGWRITING, REHEARSALS, AND JAMS

If a song can be likened to a house, then I–IV–V chords are its foundation. Even musicians who don't read music understand the term and refer to it in songwriting, rehearsals, and also jam sessions, where people play songs they may not have heard before. Someone might announce that a particular song is in the key of E. If people can figure out that the I, IV and V chords are E, A, and B, they can jump in and play along with at least a major part of the song.

NON-MUSICIANS FEEL THE POWER OF I-IV-V

People who aren't musicians have heard I–IV–V chord progressions in popular songs so often that they can sense where a verse or chorus melody is heading, even if they've never heard the song before. Commercial teen-pop songs use I–IV–V chords. The same goes with many folk, bluegrass, country, melodic punk, rock, and blues tunes. We'll play a blues next!

THE 12-BAR BLUES

Classic 12-bar blues songs are perfect for learning how to hear and play I–IV–V chord *changes* (musicians often refer to a series of chords as a *progression*, or *changes*). The blues has a set structure, which serves a purpose—to support the storytelling quality of the *lyrics* (the words sung in a song). You can also play a 12-bar blues without vocals.

This example introduces *triplets*. A triplet is three notes in the time of two, so, in an *eighth-note triplet* we play three notes in one beat instead of the usual two.

How the 12-Bar Blues Form Works

Track 64 Let's try this 12-bar blues in D.

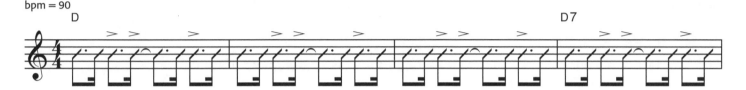

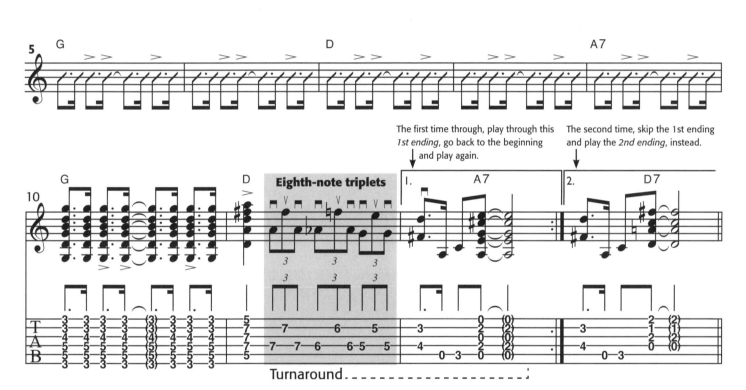

The first time through, play through this *1st ending*, go back to the beginning and play again.

The second time, skip the 1st ending and play the *2nd ending*, instead.

Turnaround

The I chord (D) is played in bars 1–3. In bar 4 it switches to a D7 (still a I chord) to build a stronger anticipation for the IV chord. The IV chord (G7) is played in bars 5–6, and we return to the I chord for bars 7–8.

The peak of the song happens in bars 9–12. The V chord (A7) comes in bar 9, followed by the IV chord in bar 10, and then I returns for bars 11–12. The V chord reappears at the very end, setting us up to play another verse or a solo over a full verse. To finish the song, end with a I chord instead (you'll hear it on the CD track.)

Turnarounds

Bars 11–12 in blues songs often include a chord passage or melodic phrase called a *turnaround*. It serves as a passage from the end of one verse into the next. The turnaround is marked in this song. There are many different kinds.

You can substitute dominant seventh chords for all the major chords to create a harder blues sound. Or, you can also play a power chord shuffle pattern from pages 27–28.

More About Riffs

There are lots of ways you can play riffs besides with power chords.

We can use expressive techniques that are also used in lead guitar playing: hammer-ons, pull-offs, bends, slides, and vibrato. We're going to learn how to do these now.

Above each example you'll see the standard abbreviations for each technique that you'd see in songbooks or guitar magazine lessons. Underneath each example you'll find the best left-hand fingering to use.

HAMMER-ONS

A *hammer-on* is an ascending *legato* (smooth and connected) technique where only the first note is picked. Pick the first note (the lower one) with your guitar pick. Hammer on the second note by tapping its fret with another finger of your fretting hand.

 Hammer-On Exercise

Track 65 Make sure your hammer-on note is as loud as the first, picked note. This takes some practice, but you can do it!

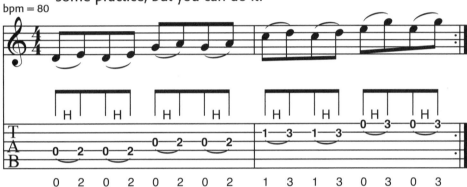

PULL-OFFS

A *pull-off* is almost the exact opposite of a hammer-on. It is a descending legato technique. Put two fretting-hand fingers down on the two notes you'll be playing. Pick the first note, then pull off to sound the second note with the other finger.

 Pull-Off Exercise

Track 66 Make sure the pulled-off note sounds as loud and clear as the first, picked note.

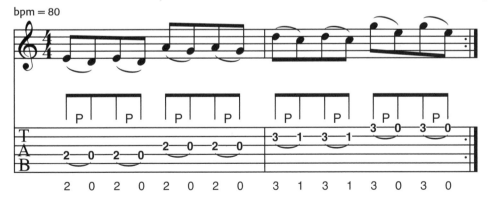

Practice hammer-ons and pull-offs on different strings and with different fingers.

BENDS

Bends have a very vocal quality to them. The string is bent up to smoothly move the pitch up to sound a *quarter step* (less than a half step) half step, whole step, one and a half step, or even higher than the fretted note. A bend is done by picking the first note and then immediately pushing the string upward toward the ceiling, or pulling it downward toward the floor, until the note reaches the desired pitch. The bigger the bend, the more your fingertips are needed to push!

Bending Upward or Downward?

When bending notes on the 1st, 2nd, 3rd, or 4th strings, use an upward motion, pushing the note up towards you. When bending a note on the 5th or 6th string, pull it downward, away from you. If you push those lower strings up, you'll push them off the fretboard.

Use Multiple Fingers, Wrist, and Thumb

You don't want to bend the notes on the top strings with just one finger! Often, your 3rd finger will be on the sounding note. Line up your middle and index fingers right behind it, so that all three fingers are on the same string. Now you've got three fingers to do the bend instead of just one, so it's much less work!

Your wrist and thumb can help out, too. As your fingers push the bending string upward, you can wrap your thumb around the neck and reach toward the other fingers, in a clawing motion.

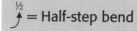
½♪ = Half-step bend

1♪ = Whole-step bend

Half and Whole Bend Exercise

Track 67 In the first bar, you're going to bend a note up a half step so that you get the exact same pitch as the note that's one fret away from it.

Once you can do a half bend, move on to the whole bends (sometimes marked ^{full}♪) in the second bar. Here, you're going to bend a note up a whole step to sound the exact same pitch as the note that's two frets away from it.

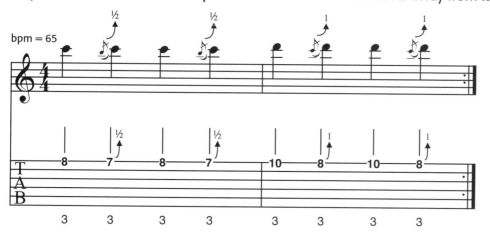

Pick, Bend, and Release

Track 68   For a *bend and release*, pick the first note, bend it up a half step, and then release the bend to smoothly straighten the string and bring the note back down to its original pitch. Since you're picking only the first note, be sure to pick it hard enough to sustain the sound through the release.

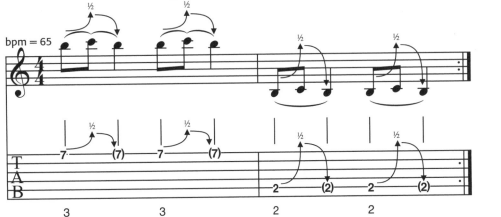

 = Bend and release

Be sure to practice half, whole, and released bends on different strings.

SLIDES

To perform a *slide*, pick the first note then slide your finger up the string until you reach the second, higher note, or down the string to a lower note for the *reverse slide*. Only the first note is picked.

Slide Exercise

Track 69   Slides can be done slow, or so fast that you can barely hear the first note. On the CD track you'll hear a slow slide first, and then a quick slide. Notice the quick slide is written with a little note called a *grace note*.

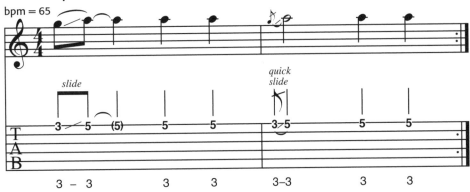

Reverse Slide Exercise

Track 70   In a reverse slide, pick the note and then slide the note down the string until you reach the second, lower note. If you play a reverse slide really fast, you can create a whining, crying sound.

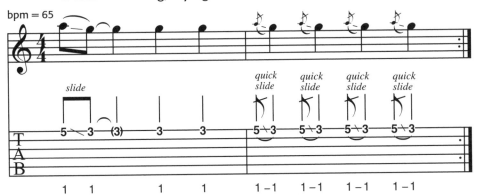

As with all the previous exercises, don't forget to try them out on all six strings.

VIBRATO

You can often tell who is playing the guitar by their use of *vibrato* (pronounced "veh-brah-toh"). Like bends, vibrato simulates a human voice. Have you ever noticed how singers end lines in a song by making the last note flutter up and down in pitch in a very subtle way? That's a vibrato. It adds warmth and life to a note, and it can give it greater *sustain* (make it last longer).

How to Create Vibrato

One way to create a vibrato—the slight flutter up and down in pitch—is to pick the note and then immediately roll your fingertip from side to side horizontally, pushing the string a little flat and then pulling it a little sharp. A vibrato can be done slow or fast, creating different effects. Another way to add vibrato to a note is with a shaking motion of the fretting hand, performing very small bends to cause the wavering of pitch.

 ### Vibrato Exercise

Track 71 Experiment with slow or fast vibrato in any riffs or lead guitar phrases you play. On the CD track, you'll hear a slow vibrato first, and then a quick one.

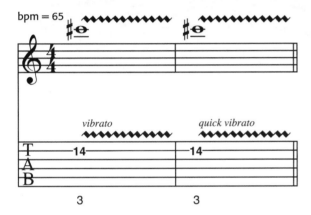

Remember: By rolling the finger back and forth in a vibrato, you're actually loosening and tightening the string to move the pitch of the note down and up. Listen carefully to make sure your vibrato note sounds good against the rest of the music (the background chords, for instance).

A vibrato can also be created using the whammy bar on your electric guitar. We'll go over how to use a whammy bar later in the lead guitar section.

A Few Words About the Riffs Coming Up Next

The following riffs are in the style of riffs from famous rock tunes. Some are intentionally played slower, just to make it easier to hear what's going on.

If you're inspired to come up with your own riffs as you're practicing, that's great! That's why the riffs were included in the book—to give you ideas and show different ways you can express a note with these techniques.

If a riff is in a style of music that isn't your favorite, try it anyway. Many times you can put your own spin on it. All these riffs include useful expressive techniques.

RIFFOLOGY: FROM FUNK TO METAL, INDIE, GLAM, ROCKABILLY, & MORE

The purpose of these riffs is to spark your own creative ideas—not to teach you note-perfect renditions of entire songs. Above each example, you'll see letters. Those are chords that go together with the riff. If you're jamming with another guitar or keyboard player, they can play the chords while you play the riff.

Below the TAB, you'll see the recommended fingering for your fretting hand.

Rock and Blues Riffs Over I–IV–V Chords

Here are two riffs where, instead of playing the chords of a I–IV–V progression, a single-note riff implying these chord changes is played.

Track 72 IN THE STYLE OF ALBERT KING'S "OH, PRETTY WOMAN (CAN'T MAKE YOU LOVE ME)"

This is a bluesy riff with subtle bends. Note the fingering used in bar 4 to get to the V chord.

Track 73 IN THE STYLE OF THE BEATLES' "DAY TRIPPER"

This one really has a 1960s pop sound. The fingering is the same for the I and IV chords, but it changes for the V chord, so follow the guide below the TAB.

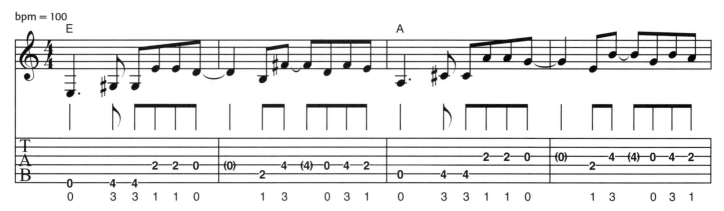

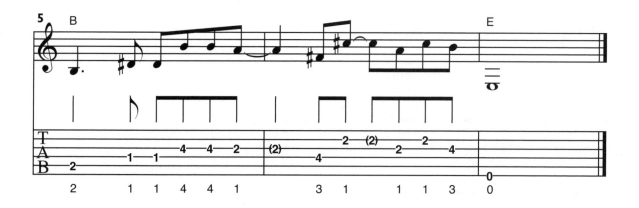

CLASSIC ROCK, HARD ROCK AND METAL RIFFS

 IN THE STYLE OF T. REX'S "20TH CENTURY BOY"
Track 74

The chord strum at the end is classic, and you'll play a bend on the 6th string.

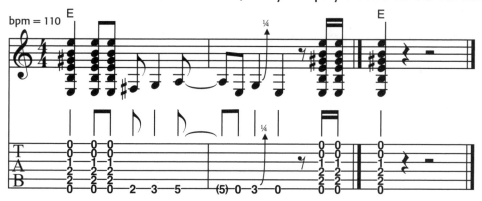

 IN THE STYLE OF JIMI HENDRIX'S "PURPLE HAZE."
Track 75

This lead guitar-style riff includes slides, vibrato and a hammer-on.

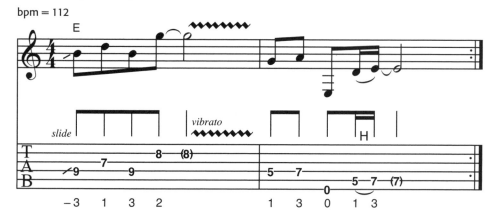

"A great rock riff: memorable, repeatable—something to be played at top volume at guitar stores."

Vickie Peterson, *guitarist, singer, songwriter (The Bangles, Continental Drifters)*

IN THE STYLE OF THE DONNAS' "FALL BEHIND ME"

Track 76

Here, you'll bend and release on two strings simultaneously.

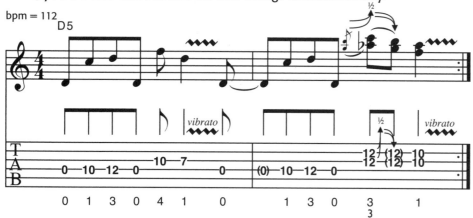

 IN THE STYLE OF PRINCE'S "LET'S GO CRAZY"

Track 77

This is a really cool line that climbs upward in half steps for a dramatic effect.

 IN THE STYLE OF DAVID BOWIE'S "REBEL REBEL"

Track 78

This one plays around notes of open chords, using pull-offs and hammer-ons.

IN THE STYLE OF BLACK SABBATH'S "SUPERNAUT"

Track 79

When you slide up the fretboard from the open 6th string, the 9th fret is an approximate place to stop—the sound effect of the slide is more important than landing on, and sounding, a particular note. Also, guitars are often tuned down a step or more in this genre (although this track is in standard tuning).

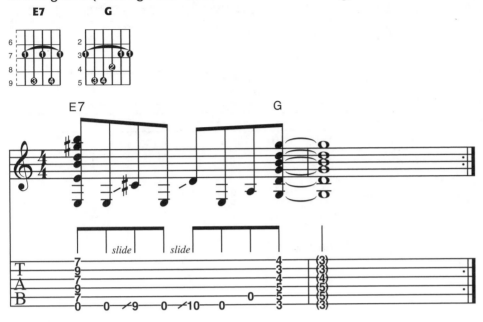

 IN THE STYLE OF GUNS N' ROSES' "SWEET CHILD O' MINE"

Track 80

Watch your fretting-hand fingering and use alternate picking! You'll play each phrase almost the exact same way (only the first note will change).

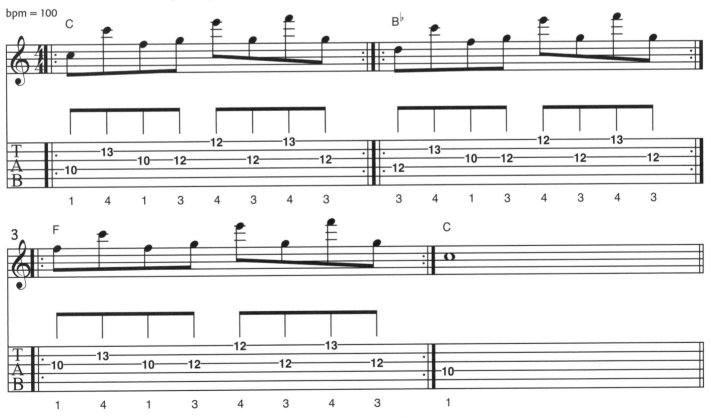

If you are you unsure of what any of the symbols above the riffs mean, go to page 56 and get an overview on bends, hammer-ons, pull-offs, slides, and vibrato. Knowing how to do these things will make the riffs sound much better.

IN THE STYLE OF IRON MAIDEN'S "THE TROOPER"

Track 81

This is an example of 1980s metal, with influences from classical music. Pull-offs and hammer-ons are very often used to play fast runs like these.

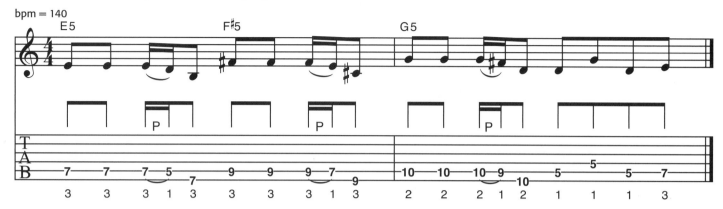

 IN THE STYLE OF METALLICA'S "THROUGH THE NEVER"

Track 82

In this thrash metal riff, the notes on the 5th string accent beats 2 and 4.

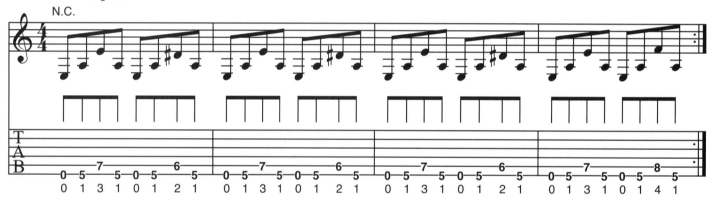

NOTE: Metal guitar styles after the 1990s usually feature drop tunings and time signatures other than $\frac{4}{4}$. Check out the DVD *Guitar World: Beginning Hard Rock & Metal!* at www.alfred.com if you want to get more into metal guitar.

FUNK ROCK RIFFS

 IN THE STYLE OF FUNKADELIC'S "HIT IT AND QUIT IT"

Track 83

Play this riff with a wah pedal if you have one (more about effects in Section 5).

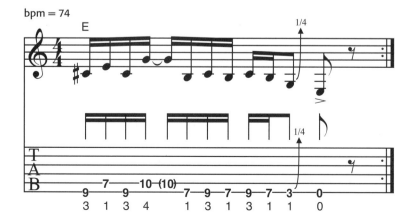

Make sure you're using the correct fingerings. It makes playing a lot easier! Always check the fingering guideline under the TAB. The numbers indicate the fingers of your fretting hand:

1 = index finger
2 = middle finger
3 = ring finger
4 = pinkie

IN THE STYLE OF BETTY DAVIS' "THEY SAY I'M DIFFERENT"

Track 84

Betty Davis was the queen of funk! This lick has bends and vibrato. It only sounds funky in relation to a beat, so use your metronome or tap your foot!

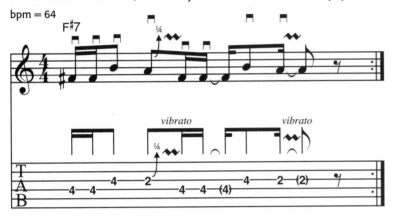

IN THE STYLE OF LENNY KRAVITZ'S "ALWAYS ON THE RUN"

Track 85

In funk guitar, it's very common to subdivide a $\frac{4}{4}$ beat into four groups of sixteenth notes, like this: "one-e-and-a, two-e-and-a, three-e-and-a, four-e-and-a." Practice funk rock riffs extremely slow at first, and keep in mind that every note and rest you play is a part of a sixteenth-note group.

Funk picking is quite a different animal: percussive, with lots of right-hand muting.

***Kat Dyson**, guitarist, singer and composer (Prince, Cyndi Lauper, P-Funk Allstars)*

ROCKABILLY

Cordell Jackson was one of the first female rockabilly guitarists. This riff is in the style of her classic "The Split" and it implies a I–IV–V chord progression. You'll be palm muting all the notes and using alternate picking.

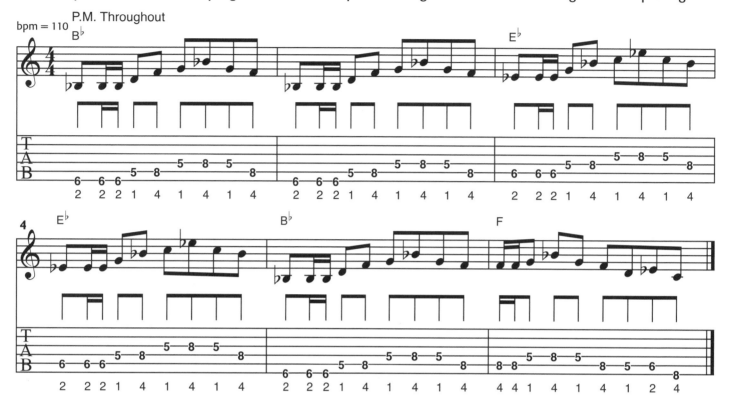

INDIE ROCK RIFFS

Some musicians say "indie rock is rarely about the riff per se, it's more about how it all fits together." Although many indie rock songs open with very memorable guitar melodies that qualify as riffs, the role of the "guitar hero"–showcasing his or her abilities through riffs and solos—doesn't exist in indie rock like it does in other rock styles.

The indie aesthetic often breaks away from the blues and country influences that are so prevalent in classic rock. This makes the sound and the role of the guitar in indie rock quite different.

One of the cool things about indie rock is that there are several female guitarists who've created the genre's most timeless songs and riffs.

 IN THE STYLE OF THE BREEDERS' "CANNONBALL"

Track 87

In this riff, you'll slide and reverse slide back and forth between four notes.

IN THE STYLE OF SLEATER-KINNEY'S "DIG ME OUT"

Track 88

In this riff, you'll play chords on two and three strings and some single notes.

 IN THE STYLE OF SONIC YOUTH'S "TEEN AGE RIOT"

Track 89

Sonic Youth usually use *alternate tunings* (see Appendix A), but you can create the dreamy feel of this riff with standard tuning. Practice the rhythm slowly.

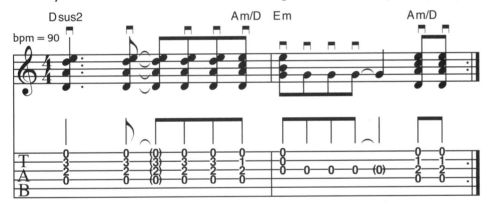

 IN THE STYLE OF MUSE'S "THOUGHTS OF A DYING ATHEIST"

Track 90

The original riff is played with a capo on the 10th fret and it's very fast. Practice its eighth-note-based rhythm slowly, and follow the picking guideline. The high notes will sound accented, but play each note with the same level of attack.

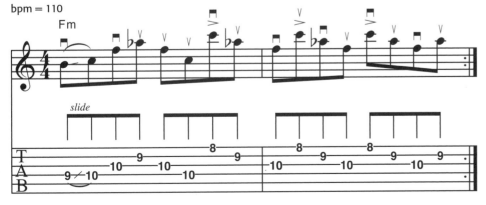

IN THE STYLE OF DEATH CAB FOR CUTIE'S "CATH..."

This riff implies the G and Cmaj7 chords, and uses slides and hammer-ons.

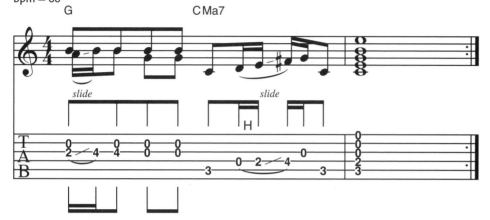

 IN THE STYLE OF THE SMITHS' "HOW SOON IS NOW?"

The original riff has two guitar parts. You'll be quiet for the first three beats, then play the sliding chord on beat 4, sustaining it over to the next bar.

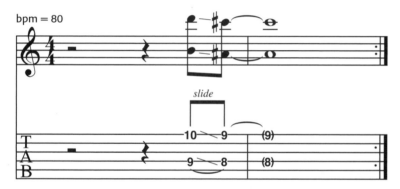

 IN THE STYLE OF RADIOHEAD'S "CREEP"

Here's a great example of arpeggio playing, where you pick the chord tones one-by-one in each chord. The D major to D minor shift is a classic songwriting trick.

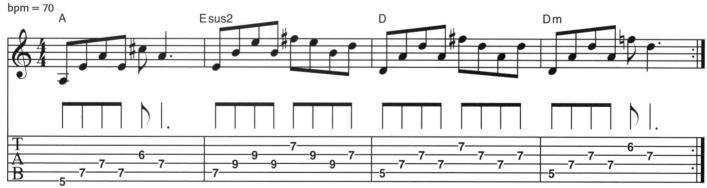

IN THE STYLE OF PJ HARVEY'S "THE LETTER"
Track 94

The original riff is played in an alternate tuning, but you'll play this one in standard tuning. To play the clicking muted notes (the x's in the second bar) just touch the 2nd string very lightly with your 1st finger without pressing it down against the fretboard.

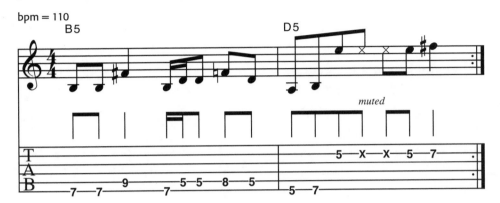

Muted Notes

Indicated with an x-shaped note-head, a *muted note* is a percussive, unpitched sound.

This sound is usally created by releasing some of the pressure from fingers playing a note or chord, but leaving them on the string to keep it from vibrating freely. Picking the string then creates a percussive sound that can create exciting rhythmic effects.

 IN THE STYLE OF THE WHITE STRIPES' "SEVEN NATION ARMY"
Track 95

This hypnotic riff is similar to a dance music hook because it's repeated over and over. It's originally played in an alternate tuning, but this version is in standard tuning.

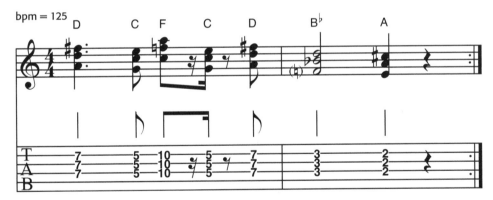

 Once you've played these riffs, try them in different keys (move them up or down the fretboard). Add different chords to them—change them. Write songs with them!

THE MOODY MINOR SONGS

Songs in *minor keys* (where the main chord is a minor chord) tend to sound darker and more melancholy because of the prominence of minor chords. One way of exploring this sound is to play a minor blues. A minor blues can use the same 12-bar song form, but the I chord is always a minor chord. Often, the IV chord is minor, too, while the V chord is either minor, major, or a dominant 7th.

 A MINOR BLUES

 Track 96

Let's try playing a common minor blues progression in A minor.

There are many variations of minor blues songs that include other chords in the last four bars. The most famous minor blues song is B.B. King's "The Thrill Is Gone." It's a really popular song to play at blues jam sessions. Try to learn it!

Minor Chords in Rock

 IN THE STYLE OF "BANG BANG (MY BABY SHOT ME DOWN)"

 Track 97

Rock is full of moody minor songs. One example is "Bang Bang (My Baby Shot Me Down)," covered by Cher, Nancy Sinatra, and The Raconteurs. Let's try playing a minor I chord (Dm); a V7 (A7), and a power chord riff.

Chords

MORE ABOUT CHORDS

A chord is two or more notes played together.

The three fundamental notes in a chord are called the root, the *3rd*, and the *5th*. They're derived from the *major scale* that shares the same letter name as the chord. A *scale* is a series of notes in a specific order of whole and half steps. The major scale is the one that sounds like "Do–Re–Mi–Fa–So–La–Ti–Do," and its specific order of steps is: whole–whole–half–whole–whole–whole–half.

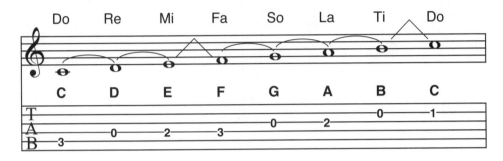

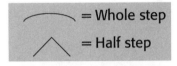

IMPORTANT NOTE: The third note of a major scale is called a *major 3rd*. The fifth note of a major scale is called a *perfect 5th*.

Track 98

Root, 3rd and 5th = Major Chord

If you stack the first, third and fifth notes of the C major scale and play them together, you get a C major chord. This is one way background singers stack notes and sing in harmony—one singer sings the root of a chord, another sings the 3rd, and another sings the 5th. Together, their voices match the chord of the song.

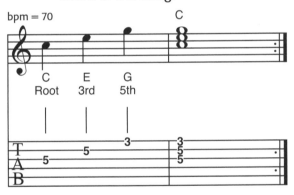

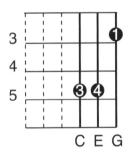

The Root

The first note of the C major chord, C, is called the root ("C" on the chord diagram.) It's the most important note, since it's the note from which the chord is constructed.

Track 99

The Major 3rd

If you start from C and count three letters forward (with "C" being "one"), you'll get the 3rd ("E" on the chord diagram.) In a C major chord, this note is E. A song to help you remember what the distance of the root to a major 3rd sounds like is the first two notes in "When the Saints Go Marching In." Listen to the CD track.

Track 100

The Perfect 5th

The 5th ("G" on the chord diagram) is five letters away from C. In a C major chord, the 5th is G. A good melody to help you remember what the distance of a root to a perfect 5th sounds like is the first two notes in "Bah, Bah, Black Sheep." Listen to what a 5th sounds like on the CD track.

The Minor 3rd

Let's lower the major 3rd, E, down a half step (one fret) to E♭. This is a *minor 3rd* (also referred to as a ♭3). You still have three letters from C to E♭, so we're still able to call this note a 3rd. But this one little shift creates a dramatically different sounding chord: a minor chord instead of a major chord. That's why the 3rd is the second most important chord tone (after the root).

Root, Minor 3rd and Perfect 5th = Minor Chord

Track 101 A minor 3rd sounds like the first two notes in the "Smoke on the Water" riff.

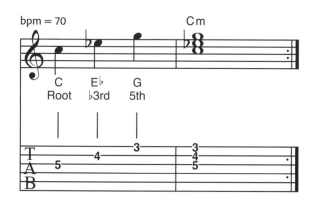

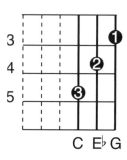

Double of Everything!

Because open or barre chords are played on four, five, or six strings, the root, 3rd, and 5th get doubled, and sometimes even tripled.

Most guitar chord shapes we play on the guitar have the root, 3rd, and 5th in a variety of arrangements, instead of neatly stacked in root–3rd–5th order. But in most of the chord types we'll cover in this book, the root *will* be the bottom note.

In the chords below, notice 1) the difference between A major and A minor, and 2) how notes are doubled and even tripled.

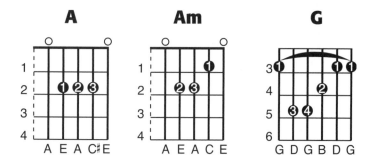

Ear Training Exercise:

Play Barre Chords, Listen for Major or Minor 3rds

Being able to distinguish between different types of chords really helps when figuring out songs.

Play a couple of major, minor, and dominant seventh barre chords. Even if you move them up and down the fretboard, the distance between the root and 3rd will look the same for each chord type. Check it out—you'll see it's true!

Now, play the root and then the 3rd in each chord. Notice if they sound like "When the Saints…" (major) or "Smoke on the Water" (minor). Then raise each chord up or down a fret or two. Notice that the 3rds still sound the same.

CHORDS THAT ADD MORE COLOR

By using other chords than just major or minor, you can add some very interesting moods and textures to your guitar style and songs. Most chords here are moveable, so just look for the root note on the 6th or 5th strings (see page 45).

Sus Chords

Sus stands for *suspended*. By raising the major 3rd in the chord one half step (one fret), you get the airy, ethereal sound of a sus4 chord (R–4–5). Lowering the 3rd a whole step makes an equally beautiful-sounding sus2 chord (R–2–5).

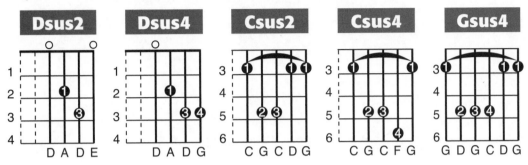

NO MORE WAR

Track 102

There are lots of sus-chords in John Lennon's and Yoko Ono's "Happy Xmas (War Is Over)." This example is in the style of that song. As usual, this $\frac{12}{8}$ is felt as a slow four beats per measure.

Major 7th Chords

Major 7th chords have a lush and sweet sound. They've appeared in Coldplay songs and hard rock classics like Thin Lizzy's "The Boys Are Back in Town." Here, the seventh note of the major scale is added to the chord's stack of root, 3rd, and perfect 5th (R–3–5–7).

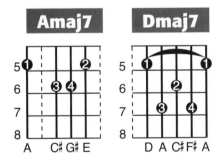

LORD KNOWS I'M DOWN

Track 103

This progression is in the style of The Smiths' "Heaven Knows I'm Miserable Now."

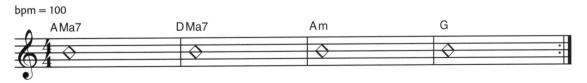

Minor Seventh Chords

If you know how to play minor barre chords, it's easy to play minor 7th barre chords, which sound smoother and a little less dark than regular minor chords. Here, the minor 7th is added to the stack of root, minor 3rd, and perfect 5th (R–♭3–5–♭7).

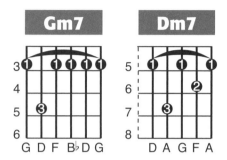

 CAT ROCKS NYC

Track 104

Try playing these minor 7th chords in the style of Cat Power's moody and very personal cover of "New York, New York."

bpm = 70

DYNAMICS — FROM QUIET TO LOUD

Let's take a short break from chords to talk about something incredibly important in music: *dynamics*. This is about how loud or soft we play. Great musicians are very aware of playing with dynamics. It makes the music breathe. When you go from a loud part to a quieter part, your return to the loud part will have a much greater impact.

In traditional classical music, the dynamic terms are in Italian. Most likely, you won't see these terms in a rock band's song chart, so here is how they translate into English:

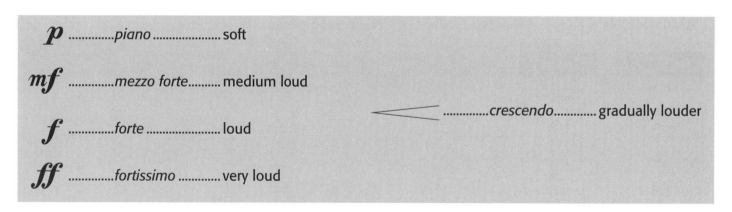

p ....piano .... soft

mf ....mezzo forte.......... medium loud

f ....forte .... loud

ff ....fortissimo .... very loud

..............crescendo............ gradually louder

 WHISPER AND SHOUT–PLAYING WITH DYNAMICS

Track 105

Start this G chord playing loud, do a dramatic shift to quiet, then build back up to loud.

bpm = 80

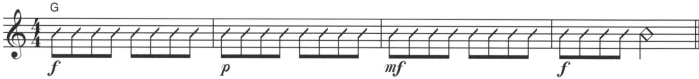

9th Chords

The *9th chord* is the ultimate funk and soul chord, so if you want to add that flavor to your rock, try it out. The 9th is the second note after the *octave*, which is eight notes higher than the root. The 9th is the same as a 2nd, but we only call a chord a 9th chord if it also has a 7th (R–3–5–♭7–9).

9th chords are often played instead of dominant 7th chords. These two versions are movable up and down the neck.

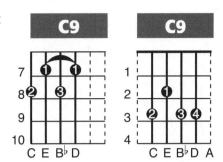

 RIVER OF SOUL

Track 106

Let's try a funk groove inspired by Susan Tedeschi's "Back to the River." Use the C9 chord on the right, above (root on the 5th string).

The typical funk rhythm is based on sixteenth notes, so the rhythm will sound something like "one, two-e-and-a!" The first beat is accented. On beat 2, the first sixteenth note is sounded. The second and third sixteenth notes are muted by the left hand to create a percussive sound. The fourth sixteenth note is sounded. Rest on beats 3 and 4 in the first bar. In the second bar, you'll play a single-note melody over those beats. Practice slowly!

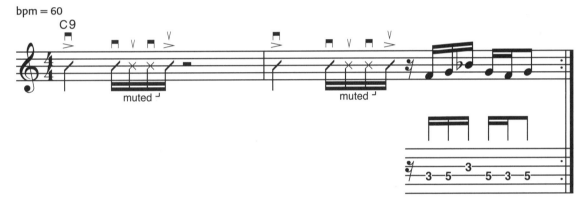

Add9 Chords

Add9 chords sound dreamy. As with the 9th chord, the 9th refers to the second note following the octave. The difference here is there is no 7th. In Southern rock, country, and acoustic music, a Cadd9 is often played instead of an open C chord. The second example on the right is movable up and down the neck.

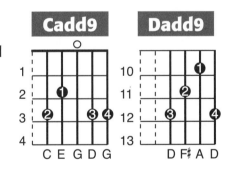

 SHE'S GOT FIRE

Track 107

Let's try playing moveable add9 chords in the style of Jimi Hendrix's "Fire."

bpm = 120

7th Augmented 9th Chords

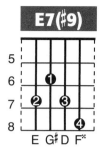

The 7th augmented 9th chord—usually called 7(♯9) for short—raises the 9th up a half step. It's common in bluesy rock, where it is played as the V chord (instead of a dominant 7th chord). Jimi Hendrix popularized it in songs like "Purple Haze" and "Foxy Lady," so it's often nicknamed "the Hendrix chord." Notice that ♯9 in an E7(♯9) chord is a *double sharp* (✕), which means the note is raised a whole step. The 9th in an E major scale is F♯, so to make it a ♯9, the F has to be double sharped.

The Sound of an E7(♯9) Chord—the "Jimi Hendrix Chord"

Track 108

Go back to the minor blues exercise (page 70) and play E7(♯9) instead of E. It sounds pretty cool, doesn't it? You can also use it as the V chord in a major key blues in A, or as the I chord in a song in the key of E.

More About Slash Chords

We explored how a string of chords can create a walking bass line on page 36, and discussed slash chords briefly on that page.

Remember, a slash chord is a chord that has a note other than the root in the *bass* (lowest note). The chord is written to the left of the slash sign, while the new bass note is written to the right of the slash sign. For example, a D/F♯ chord is D major with an F♯ in the bass.

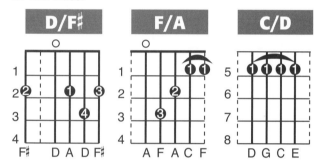

In rock, slash chords are mostly used when the specific bass note is important. A typical situation is a chord progression with a descending bass line built in, like G–G/F♯–Em (the bass line being G–F♯–E). Sometimes it can add some sophistication to a chord progression. It's much more interesting, for instance, to play G–G/F♯–Em than just G to Em. The song may call for something more than a simple chord change.

 FISH ON A RIFT

Track 109

Let's play a chord progression with slash chords inspired by Phish's "Rift." Although the bass notes (F♯–A–D–C) aren't moving in gradual steps, they give the D, F, and C chords interesting colors. It ends with a basic C chord.

bpm = 100

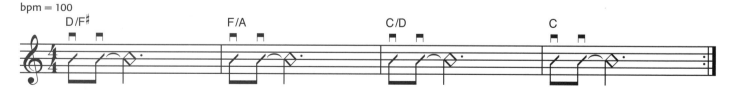

Jam Tracks: Putting Your Rhythm Guitar Skills Together

Here's your opportunity to try out what you've learned in five play-along tracks! You'll get to play in a variety of styles: classic rock, indie rock, classic metal, and two style hybrids—jam band/slow funk and new wave/ska.

Each track has two versions: one with guitar and one where the guitar is removed, so you can play along with just bass and drums. Tackle one section at a time. Make sure to look out for any repeat signs in the sections!

CLASSIC ROCK JAM

Track 110
+ guitar

Track 111
- guitar

bpm = 70

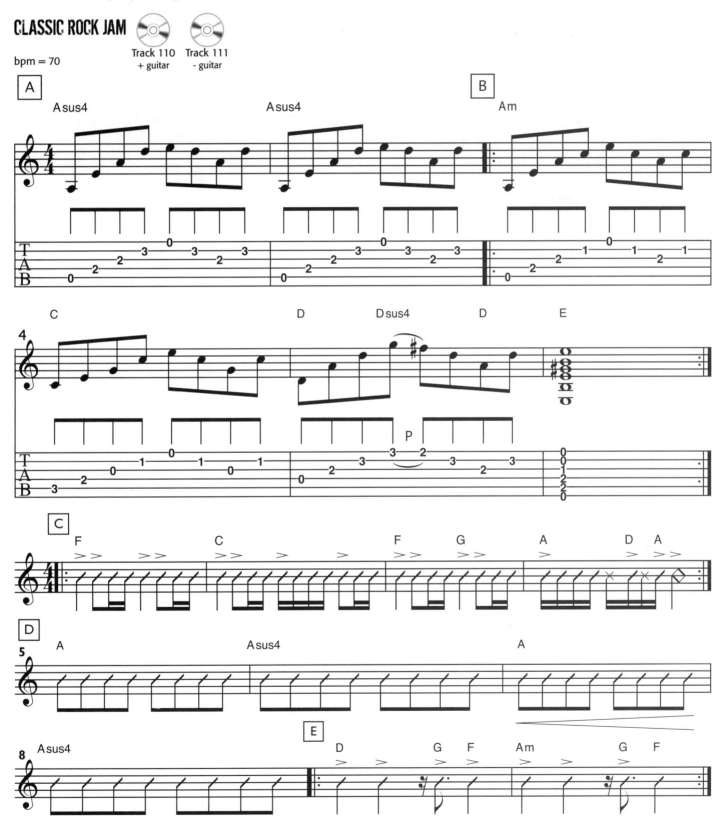

Suggested lead guitar scales: A minor pentatonic for sections B and C; D minor pentatonic for section E.

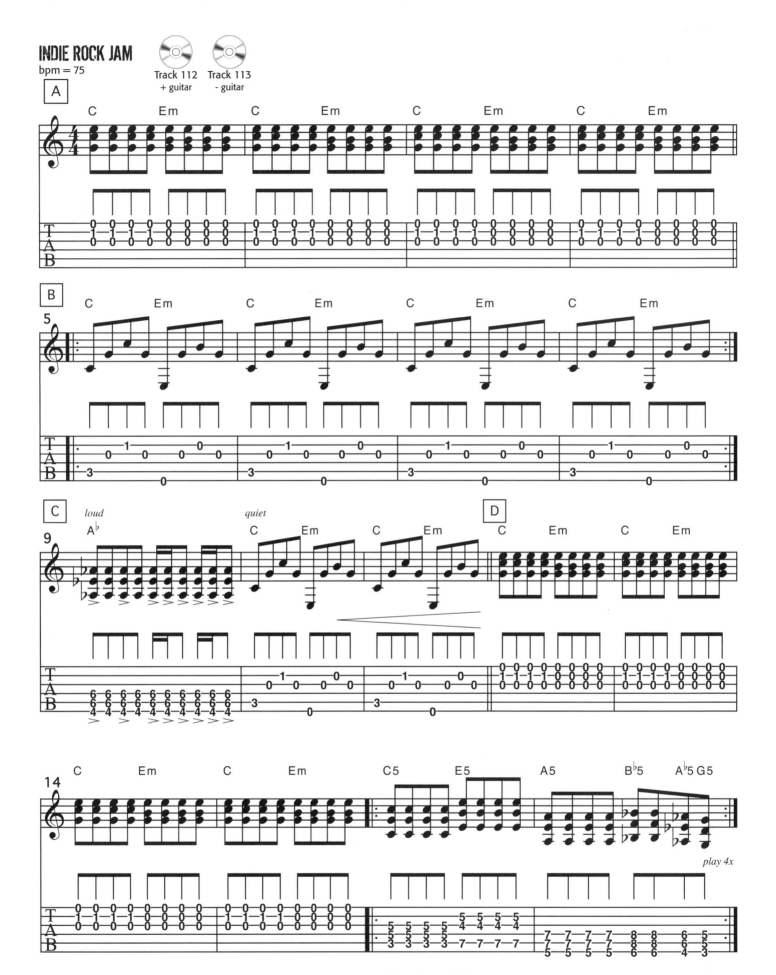

Suggested lead guitar scale: C major scale for sections A, B, and D.

NOTE: The C major scale has some notes that sound great over the E, A, and G chords but it also has some *dissonant* (clashing) notes. Sometimes, however, dissonance is a desired effect, so listen and experiment! If a note sounds "wrong" to you, there's always a more pleasing note just one fret above or below. You can also bend dissonant notes up to the "right" pitch if you like.

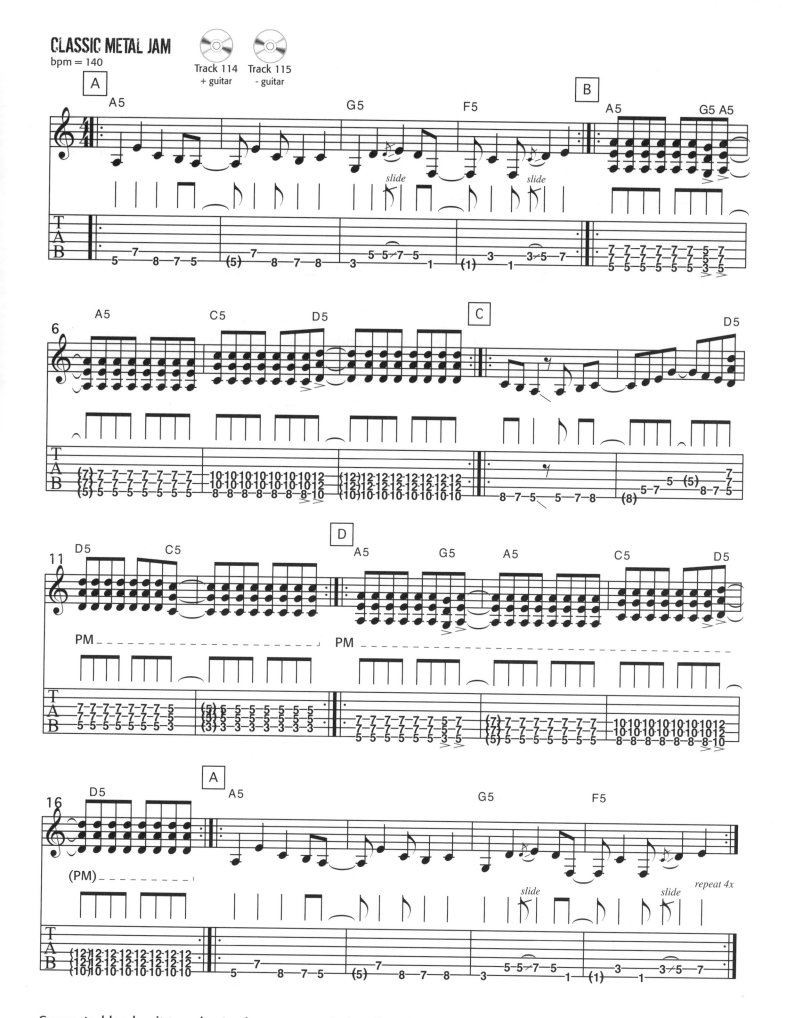

Suggested lead guitar scale: A minor pentatonic for all sections; the A natural minor scale for sections A and D.

JAM BAND/SLOW FUNK JAM
bpm = 75

Track 116 + guitar   Track 117 - guitar

Suggested lead guitar scales: C minor pentatonic for sections A, B, C, and D; A minor pentatonic for section E.

NOTE: When you play over sections A and D, as well as the C7 and G7 chords in section C, it will work better if you raise the second note in the C minor pentatonic scale (E♭) up one fret to an E. This way, you'll make a more major sound and sound less dissonant. You can also bend the E♭ up a half step to E.

NEW WAVE/SKA JAM

bpm = 130

Track 118
+ guitar

Track 119
- guitar

Suggested lead guitar scales: C major for sections A, B, and E; A minor pentatonic for sections C and D.

"I think being able to break down chord progressions to I–IV–V or whatever it is, is the difference between memorizing random chords and understanding the commonality in all songs."

Jennifer Batten, guitarist and composer (Michael Jackson, Jeff Beck, solo artist)

"I played with drum machines constantly. I write a lot of music and I would develop drum patterns, record them on a little 4-track, and play to that. You have to be in time! Before that, as a kid, I would play into a cassette and jam with myself, so I had to be sure my time was good since I wasn't playing alone, so to speak. And since I've been in NY, I've been unbelievably lucky to play with incredible drummers."

Ann Klein, guitarist, mandolin/dobro/lap steel player, singer, composer (Ani DiFranco, Joan Osborne, various Broadway shows, solo artist)

"When I play a blues shuffle, I cue in on the drummer. That's where the feel is; hi-hat and snare drive the feel, and the bass drum locks it in."

Kat Dyson, guitarist, singer and composer (Prince, Cyndi Lauper, P-Funk Allstars)

YOU MADE IT!

You've arrived at the end of the rhythm guitar section. Congratulations!

You've gained many skills when it comes to chords, rhythms, riffs, and the use of silence, space and dynamics. You've got more knowledge about playing different styles of rock. All these things will make you a great and valuable rhythm guitarist.

Remember: Most of what a guitarist does in songs is play rhythm guitar. And when you do, you have a lot of power to make a song, singer, or soloist sound great. Your influence also extends beyond the stage—you can wow an audience because out of all the elements in music, people tend to have the strongest emotional response to rhythm.

Now let's move on into the wild world of lead guitar…

Section 3: Lead Guitar Soloing

THE FIRST FEMALE LEAD GUITARISTS

Lead guitar, which, as discussed on page 15, often is about imrovising solos, is part of the art of the electric guitar. Let's acknowledge two of the earliest electric guitar players: Memphis Minnie and Sister Rosetta Tharpe. These incredibly cool women were performing, making records, and playing solos before many male blues and rock icons did, and they were there way before the "guitar gods" of the classic rock era.

Memphis Minnie

Born in Algiers, Louisiana on June 3, 1897, Memphis Minnie was the biggest female blues singer during the Depression years and one of the first blues artists to take up the electric guitar. She paved the way for Muddy Waters and other blues legends who left their rural hometowns to make it in the big cities. After learning how to play guitar and banjo as a child, Minnie ran away from home at age 13 and joined a circus.

She released hundreds of recordings, including "When the Levee Breaks" (famously covered by Led Zeppelin). She was highly respected among her peers for her solid musicianship. When she passed away in 1973, another groundbreaking female guitarist, Bonnie Raitt, paid for the headstone at her burial site in Walls, Mississippi.

Photo Courtesy of Delta Haze Corp.

Photo Courtesy of Delta Haze Corp.

Sister Rosetta Tharpe

Born in Cotton Plant, Arkansas, on March 20, 1915, Sister Rosetta Tharpe became a huge gospel recording star in the 1930s and '40s, with hits like "Up Above My Head." Very early on, she mixed spiritual lyrics with rock 'n' roll rhythms, and she was a major influence on Aretha Franklin and Elvis Presley.

When Rosetta was only four years old, she performed as "Little Rosetta Nubin, the Singing and Guitar Playing Miracle" with her evangelist mother. In private, she played blues and jazz. Her guitar style was influenced by Memphis Minnie and a variety of jazz musicians. In the 1960s, there was a blues revival in the U.K., which inspired the upcoming generation of British classic rock bands. Her tour there fueled a new interest in her music.

Sister Rosetta Tharpe passed away in 1973, depressed by her mother's death and suffering from diabetes and a leg amputation. At first, she was buried in an unmarked grave, but in 2008 a concert was held to raise funds for a gravestone, and it was finally put in place.

FRETBOARD 101 — FINDING YOUR WAY ON THE GUITAR

If you're new to soloing, make sure you have mastered all of the material on pages 56–59 before digging into this section.

If you're a more experienced lead guitarist or you're willing to go deeper into skills like fretboard basics, how several important lead guitar scales work, and how to solo with them across the fretboard and in different keys, then you're in the right place! Grab your guitar and read on.

"I think it's crucial to know your way around the fretboard. Learn it, study it, practice until it feels natural— and then forget about it and just play."

Vicki Peterson, guitarist, singer, songwriter
(The Bangles, Continental Drifters)

The Five Octave Patterns in C

All the notes on a guitar fretboard can be organized into five different *octave patterns*. An octave pattern is the shape created on the fretboard by locating a note and finding its closest octave on another string. For example, finding C on the 5th string and then its octave version on the 2nd string, or the 4th string. Just as piano players learn the location of every C note on the keyboard, we guitar players can learn the location of every C note on the fretboard with these octave patterns.

Below are the five octave patterns for the note C. Some patterns include two C's, others include three C's. After you've played through all five patterns, they'll repeat again in the same order until we run out of frets.

Grab your guitar and play every note C. Notice which strings are involved in each pattern, whether there's a two-fret or three-fret distance between the C's, and how all the patterns overlap each other.

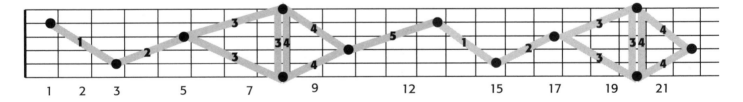

 Use your 1st and 3rd fingers for the patterns that have a two-fret distance between the notes, and your 1st and 4th fingers for the patterns with a three-fret distance.

Exercise: Octave Patterns in A

Let's move on to the next exercise and play all the A's on the guitar instead of C. We'll be starting with a different pattern (the second one), but otherwise the order sequence is the same.

We've filled in octave pattern 2 at the open 5th string and at the 3rd string, 2nd fret to get you started. Find the rest yourself and mark them in the diagrams by drawing circles (remember the patterns overlap each other). Once you've filled them in, check your work against the diagram at the bottom of the page and play them.

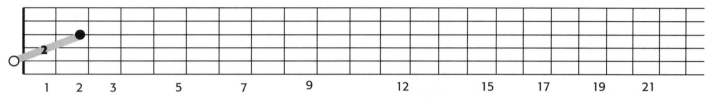

What's the Point of Knowing Octave Patterns?

Knowing the octave patterns gives you the best big-picture view of how the fretboard works. This helps you find your way around the guitar and helps you feel more in control when you play solos instead of feeling lost in a maze of strings and frets. Learning them is time well spent.

You've learned the octave patterns in C and A. This will be of great help to you when you practice the lead guitar scales in C and Am on the next pages of this book.

Playing Hendrix-Style Octaves in Solos

Melody phrases (a.k.a. "licks") that are played in octaves are also cool to use in riffs and soloing. You can hear them in rock guitar parts by Jimi Hendrix and John Frusciante, and by jazz guitarists like Wes Montgomery and the late, great Emily Remler. Let's try playing something in the style of the Red Hot Chili Pepper's "Blood Sugar Sex Magik."

 SUGARY, SEXY, MAGICAL (PLAYING OCTAVE LICKS)
Track 120

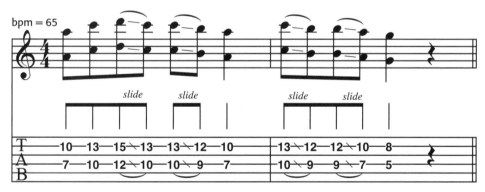

Exercise: Octave Patterns in A Answers
Turn the book upside down to see the answers.

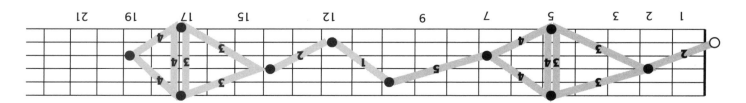

THE MAJOR SCALE

As you learned on page 71, a scale is a series of notes in alphabetical order with a specific pattern of whole and half steps. Songwriters use scale tones when they write melodies, and guitarists use them for solos. If you have ever sung "Do–Re–Mi–Fa–So–La–Ti–Do", you have sung the major scale. It's the most important scale for a rock musician to know, and often works well in non-bluesy indie rock, pop, folk, country, and soul.

The major scale is a series of eight notes ascending in alphabetical order. The major scale is the one that sounds like "Do–Re–Mi–Fa–So–La–Ti–Do," and its specific order of steps is:

Whole–Whole–Half–Whole–Whole–Whole–Half

Memorizing this will make it easy to use in any key. Remember, on the guitar, a half step equals one fret, and a whole step equals two frets.

Playing the Major Scale in C on One String

Let's play a major scale starting from the note C. We'll play it on just the 2nd string, so that you can see the pattern of whole steps and half steps.

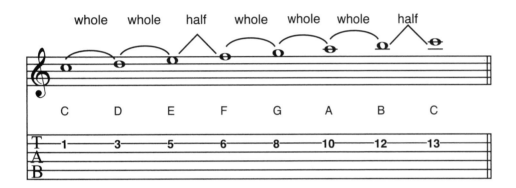

Track 121
Soloing in C Major on One String
Yes! You can play a solo on one string! The chords above the music are suggestions. Hammer-ons, slides, bends and vibrato are covered on page 56.

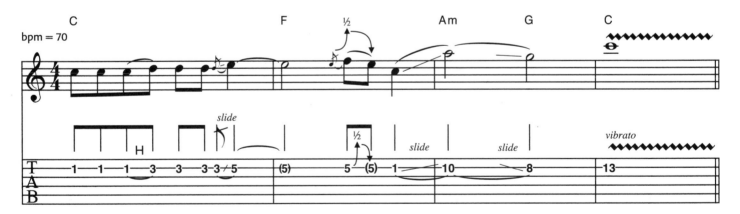

86   Womens' Road to Rock Guitar

FIVE MAJOR SCALE PATTERNS

You've just played a solo in C major on one string. Now, as you move on to playing across the strings, you'll run into scale diagrams. The diagrams you read on pages 46, 84, and 85 were the same sort of thing.

How to Read a Scale Diagram for Guitar

A scale diagram is like a snapshot of a guitar fretboard, zooming in on five specific frets (the fret numbers are indicated below).

The dots show the scale pattern. Play each note in the pattern one at a time. Start at the lowest note (lowest string) and work your way up (from left to right); then play the scale backwards (highest string to lowest, from right to left). The numbers inside the dots indicate which fretting finger plays the note. White dots at the left indicate open strings.

Let's practice the first of our five major scale patterns in C.

Pattern 1: Great with Open Chords

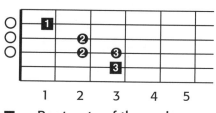

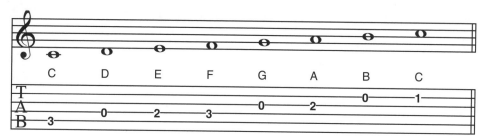

■ = Root note of the scale

When to Play This Scale

It works great if you're playing open chord versions of C, Dm, Em, F, G, Am, and B diminished* (chords in the key of C). You can easily use this scale pattern to play solo fills between the chords, bass lines between chords, and riffs.

Before practicing the licks made from it, run through the scale pattern. It will make your fingers stronger and more nimble, which is important for the licks and string bends. Plus, it will help you play licks with the optimum fingering, which makes it easier and quicker to find the notes.

Also, get in the habit of practicing all your scales and licks with alternate picking (page 13). It might feel awkward at first if you're used to picking with all downstrokes but it's worth the effort. Your playing will sound much more fluid. You'll be able to play faster lines too, with less strain on your picking arm.

"Fretboard knowledge is beyond important—it is vital! The fretboard is your playing field, your canvas to paint melodic vision. It has endless possibilities if you just get in there and spend time exploring."

Kat Dyson, *guitarist, singer and composer (Prince, Cyndi Lauper, P-Funk Allstars)*

* The B diminished chord includes the notes B, D, and F. Use a chord dictionary (Alfred Music #33501) to learn diminished chords in every key.

Patterns 2-5: Great with Barre Chords and Power Chords

Moving on up the fretboard! No more open strings! Try the C major scale at the far left.

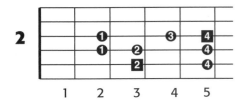

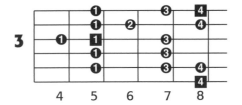

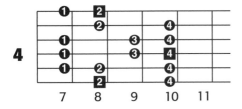

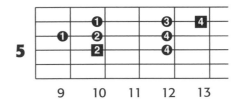

Indie Rock Lick in C with the Second Pattern

Track 122

Pattern 2 of the C major scale is nice and close to the barred C and G chords that start at the 3rd fret. Let's use it for soloing and try out this indie rock-inspired lick.

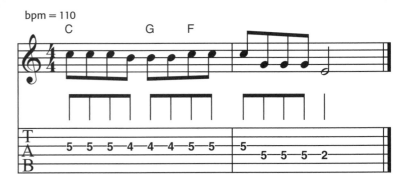

Rock Solo in C

Track 123

Play the chords along with the track and then try the solo. It uses notes from scale pattern 4, between the 7th and 10th frets. If you're playing a rhythm guitar part with a C barre chord starting at the 8th fret and it's time to play a solo, this is the closest C major scale pattern.

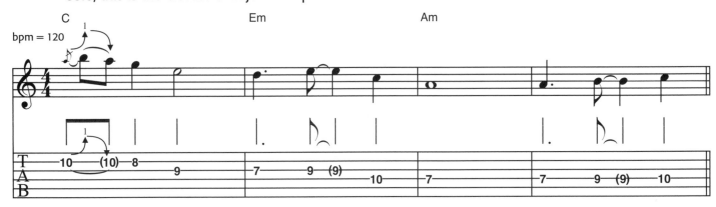

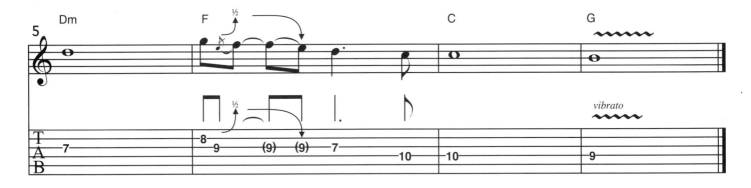

CHORDS THAT SOUND GOOD WITH THE C MAJOR SCALE

As we checked out the first C major scale pattern, we learned about the chords in the key of C: C, Dm, Em, F, G, Am, and B diminished. They'll sound great with this scale.

The C, F and G chords are called the primary chords. It's important to remember the primary chords—I–IV–V—too (page 53). In the key of C, the I–IV–V chords are C–F–G.

The Am (vi) is the most used minor chord in the key of C, followed by Em (iii).

Famous Rock Songs in C

Next to playing with other people, there's no better way to learn guitar than by jamming along with recordings. If you don't have a band yet, the amazing bands who recorded the songs on the list below will back you up with guitars, bass, drums, and maybe even keyboards as you practice your lead guitar chops. These songs are all in the key of C, so put those C major scales to use.

"Hold On"....................Alabama Shakes

"Stars"..........................Grace Potter & The Nocturnals

"Use Somebody"......Kings of Leon

"Ho Hey"....................The Lumineers

"Dy'er Maker"............Led Zeppelin

"Ruby Tuesday" ....The Rolling Stones

"Let It Be"..................The Beatles

 Quick Tip

Another way you can practice soloing is by playing along to jam tracks, a.k.a backing tracks. These are instrumental tracks (no vocals) that are created by musicians for other musicians to practice their scales, licks, and *improvisation* (spontaneous soloing) skills.

On page 77, you'll find five great jam tracks in different rock styles. They are there to help you practice soloing with the scales you'll learn in this book. Also, check out Alfred's *Classic Rock Tracks* by Chris Amelar, Robert Brown, and Allon A. Sams, and there are several rock books in Alfred's *Stand Alone* series. You can also find jam tracks on the Internet: just type "rock jam tracks in the key of C," for instance, and pick one of the many that people have posted.

WRAPPING UP — OCTAVES AND MAJOR SCALES ARE CONNECTED

You've played the five major scale patterns in C. Maybe you noticed that patterns 1, 2, and 5 have two C's and patterns 3 and 4 have three C's. Also, all five patterns overlap. And once you've played through the five patterns, the sequence will repeat until you run out of frets. But wait a minute… didn't you hear about that stuff earlier in the book?

Turn back to page 87–88 and look at the five C major scale patterns again. The C notes are highlighted in each pattern. Notice how the C's form the same five octave patterns that you learned on page 84. That's right, they're all connected!

CHANGING KEYS — IT'S EASY AND QUICK ON GUITAR

It's easy to play the C major scale patterns from page 88 in different keys. Since they don't have open strings, you can move them up or down the frets, just like a barre chord or power chord.

To play the scales in D instead of C, move them up two frets. To play them in B instead of C, move them down one fret. Just make sure you move the chords too!

Indie Rock Lick in C Moved Up to D

Track 124

Let's take the Indie Rock Lick in C from page 88 and move it up two frets. Now you're in the key of D! The I–IV–V chords in the key of D are D, G, and A.

bpm = 110

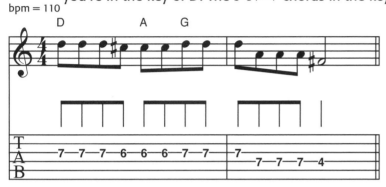

Keep practicing C major on one string. Solo on one string over the rock songs in C listed on page 89. Use slides, bends, hammer-ons, and vibrato in your solos (pages 56–59). Next, work with the five major scale patterns in C. Later on, you can try a new key like D by raising your scales (patterns 2–5) and barre chords up two frets.

And now it's time to move on to our second rock soloing scale.

THE NATURAL MINOR SCALE

If the bright, upbeat major scale had a pensive and moody sister, it would be the *natural minor scale*. We call the major scale and natural minor scale *relative scales* because they share the same notes.

The natural minor scale sounds good in songs that center around minor chords. You can write cool riffs with this scale. The Go-Go's "This Town" and R.E.M.'s "Losing My Religion" are two rock songs where the melodies, chords, and riffs sound very "natural minor."

C Major and A Minor–Related Scales

As stated above, the C major and the A natural minor scales are related. They don't sound similar, but they share the same notes. The only difference is their starting note. The natural minor scale always starts one and a half step lower than its related major scale. The note A is one and a half steps behind the note C (A to B is a whole step, B to C is a half step).

The C major scale notes: C D E F G A B C

The A natural minor scale notes: A B C D E F G A

Playing the Natural Minor Scale in A on One String

Let's play a natural minor scale starting from the note A. We'll play it on just the 3rd string, starting at the 2nd fret.

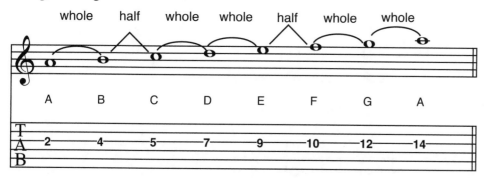

Soloing in A Minor on One String

Track 125

CHORDS THAT SOUND GOOD WITH THE NATURAL MINOR SCALE IN A

Since the C major and and its relative minor key, A minor, share the same notes, they also share they same chords in a different order: Am, Bdim (diminished), C, Dm, Em, F, and G. You can play the A natural minor scale over these. But the most played chord in a song in A minor is Am, followed by the other minor chords Dm and Em (as in track #125.)

FIVE NATURAL MINOR SCALE PATTERNS

Now that you've played a solo in A minor on one string, it's time to play across the strings!

Pattern 1: Great with Open Chords

Follow the indicated fretting-hand fingerings. Begin with the first note (A) on the open 5th string, the next note (B) with your 2nd finger on the 5th string, etc.

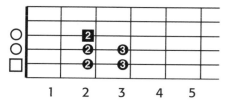

When to Play this Scale

It works great if you're playing open chord versions of Am, Bdim, C, Dm, Em, F, and G (chords in the key of A minor). You can use it for playing solo fills or walking bass lines between chords. The low notes—especially when played with bends—sound perfect for riffs.

Patterns 2–5: Great with Barre/Power Chords; Moveable to Different Keys

Here are the four moveable scale patterns. Try pattern 3, starting at the 6th string, 5th fret.

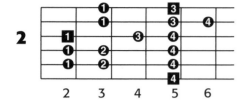

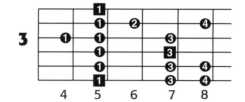

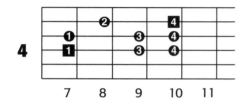

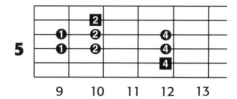

Solo Lick in the Style of The Go-Go's' "This Town"

Track 126

The A natural minor scale you just played is close to the barred Am chord at the 5th fret. Let's try some solo licks inspired by The Go-Go's' lead guitarist Charlotte Caffey.

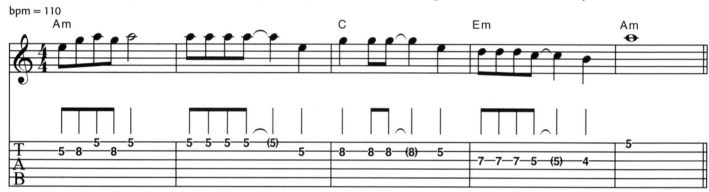

Wrap up time! Play the octave patterns shown with squares in each scale pattern at the top of this page. Try the moveable scales and the "Solo Lick in the Style of the Go-Go's' 'This Town'" in G minor by lowering it two frets.

"I think you need to learn the tools in any creative art whether your understanding is intuitive or studied. The better you know the fretboard, the more freedom you have to work your ideas into any part of the neck."

Jennifer Batten, *guitarist and composer (Michael Jackson, Jeff Beck, solo artist)*

THE MINOR PENTATONIC SCALE

As a rock lead guitarist, you'll be playing many licks from the *minor pentatonic scale*. This and the major scale are by far the most popular rock scales. The minor pentatonic sounds perfect for classic rock, blues, bluesy indie rock, funk, hard rock, metal, and even some modern jazz, reggae, R&B, and soul music.

The minor pentatonic scale is very closely related to the natural minor scale.

> Minor Pentatonic = Natural Minor without notes 2 and 6

The minor pentatonic scale only has five notes (the Greek word *penta* means five). It's simply a natural minor scale without notes 2 and 6. Let's compare the two scales, so you can see for yourself.

The A natural minor scale notes: A B C D E F G A

The A minor pentatonic scale notes: A   C D E   G A

> One good way to memorize A minor pentatonic is "the first three letters of the band AC/DC + EG."

Playing the Minor Pentatonic Scale in A on One String

Let's play a minor pentatonic scale starting from the note A. We'll play it on just the 3rd string, starting at the 2nd fret. Notice the larger steps between the notes A–C and E–G.

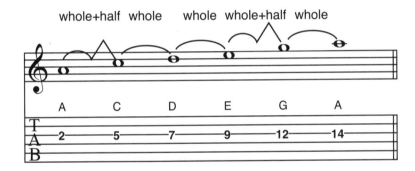

Soloing with A Minor Pentatonic on One String

Track 127

The chords above the music are just suggestions. If you don't know techniques like slides and bends, go to page 56–59 and get familiar with all of them before playing these exercises.

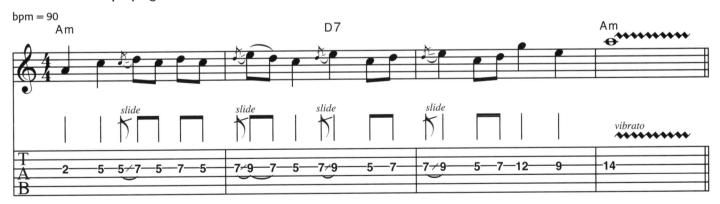

Rock Soloing with the Five Minor Pentatonic Scale Patterns in A

Now you'll be soloing in A minor pentatonic across the strings, up and down the fretboard! Many of the licks you're about to learn are classic, immortalized by male and female guitar heroes on countless inspirational rock 'n' roll albums.

All five minor pentatonic patterns in A have the same notes, A, C, D, E, and G, but the starting note is different for each pattern. Playing the patterns this way allows you to play much more interesting licks and you won't leave any strings out.

If this confuses you, start by playing the scales from A to the next A (squares).

Pattern 1 in Open Position Starting from E—Great with Open Chords

At this part of the fretboard, the A minor pentatonic scale includes several open strings. In fact, it starts with the open 6th string, which is E.

This pattern sits close to open chords like A, D, and E. Its low notes are perfect for riffs. Play the octave pattern in A first (the notes shown with squares), then the scale, and then the licks below.

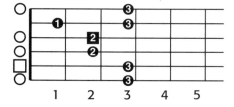

Licks with Hammer-Ons, Pull-Offs, Slides and Bends

Use your ring finger to play the hammer-ons and the very subtle, quarter-step bends.

 Minor Pentatonic Hammer-On and Bend

Track 128

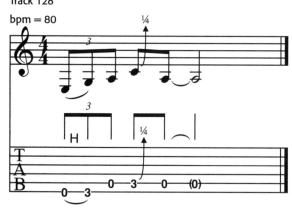

 Minor Pentatonic Hammer-On and Bend Variation

Track 129

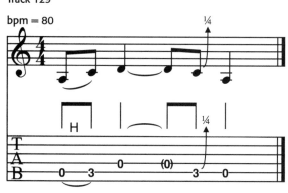

Minor Pentatonic Pull-Off and Hammer-On

Track 130 — Make sure that your hammer-on and pull-off notes sound as loud as your picked notes.

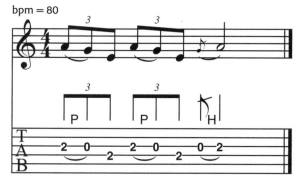

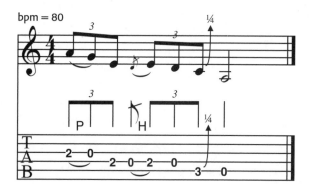

Let's Add a Bend

Track 131

Slide Lick

Track 132 — Use your 3rd finger to slide quickly from the 1st fret to the 3rd fret on the 2nd string.

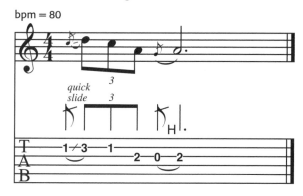

Whole Step Bend

Track 133 — With your 2nd and 1st fingers right next to it, place your fretting-hand 3rd finger on the 2nd string, 3rd fret. Bend the string up towards you with all three fingers locked together in one single motion, so that the pitch goes up a whole step (see bending demonstration on page 57). Keep holding on to the string as you slowly release the bend to its initial pitch.

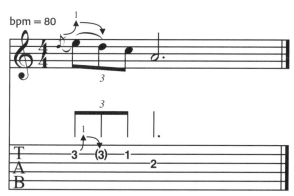

Pattern 2 on Frets 2–5: Adding Higher Notes

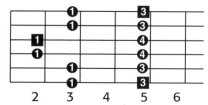

Now we'll get to expand our soloing palette by going a little higher up on the fretboard. This is the second A minor pentatonic pattern, which starts from the note G.

You get to play some very cool, bluesy rock licks with this pattern, and also combine them with the previous A minor pentatonic licks you've already played. Play the octave pattern first, then the scale, then the licks.

Slide with the 1st Finger

Track 134   Use your 1st finger to play the quick slide from the 3rd fret to the 5th fret on the 5th string.

Slide with the 3rd Finger

Track 135   Use your 3rd finger to play the quick slide that starts off this lick.

NOTE: Many guitarists prefer to use their 3rd finger to play the notes at the 5th fret on the 3rd and 4th strings; others use their 4th finger (as shown in the scale diagram).

Slide with Two Strings

Track 136   This is a bluesy lick, with a strong triplet rhythm. Start it off with a quick slide from one fret below, and finish it with a downward, tapered-off slide.

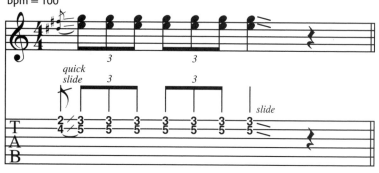

Combining Patterns 1 and 2 in Solos

Here are two licks and a solo that combine the two A minor pentatonic patterns you've learned so far. Your lowest notes will be on the open strings, and your highest notes at the 5th fret.

Hammer-Ons and Pull-Offs

Track 137

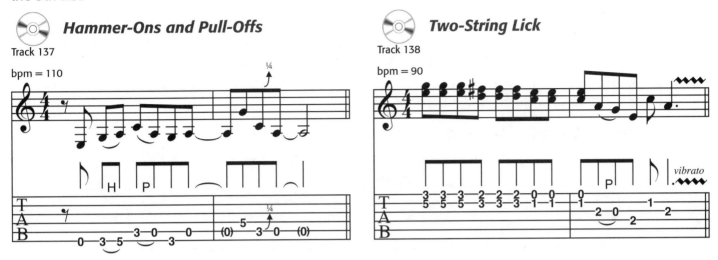

Two-String Lick

Track 138

12-Bar Blues Solo in A

Track 139

Get ready for this 12-bar blues solo by practicing the two scale patterns first. The next step is to listen to the track several times. Finally, practice the solo slowly, one lick at a time. It's a good idea to play this with a shuffle feel (see page 27).

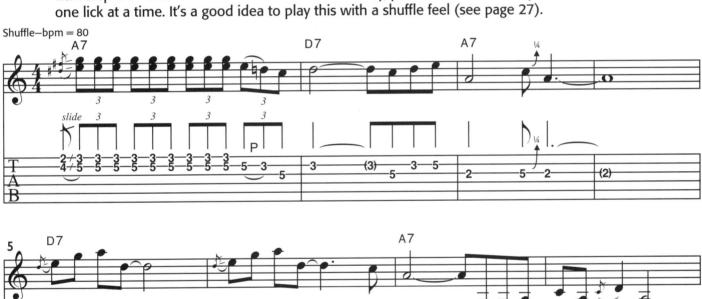

Pattern 3 on Frets 5–8 and Warm-Ups: The Most Popular Rock Scale Pattern

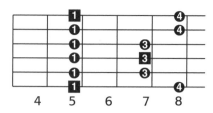

Pattern 3 starts from the note A. It's the most popular way of playing A minor pentatonic—the quintessential rock scale pattern!

It's symmetrical and easy for the fingers to memorize. The fact that it starts from A (the root note) makes it easy to play in different keys. To play it in G, start it at the 3rd fret. To play in D, start it at the 10th fret.

Here are two warm-ups with this pattern to make your fingers limber. Many rock guitarists use bits of scale runs like these in solos. Play them with alternate picking.

Pattern 3 Warm-Up with Eighth Notes

Track 140
bpm = 80

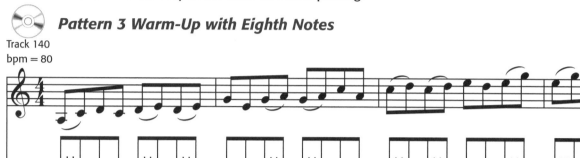

Warm-Up with Triplets

Track 141
bpm = 80

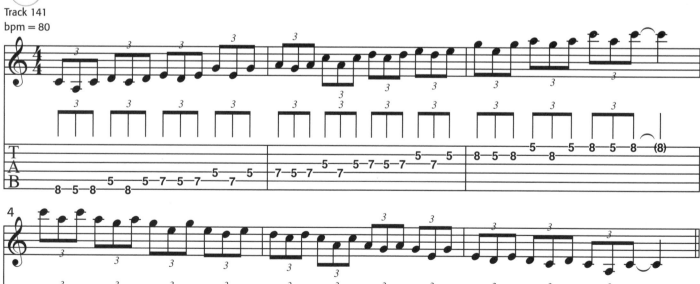

Practicing Pentatonic Soloing Licks

Play the octave pattern first (the three square notes in the scale diagram on page 98).
Then play the scale and warm-ups making sure your fingerings are correct. After that, go
for the licks! Follow the picking guidelines above each lick.

Lick with Pull-Offs

Track 142   Play this lick slowly at first and gradually increase the speed. Some guitarists do
the pull-offs with the 3rd finger instead of the 4th. Try it both ways.

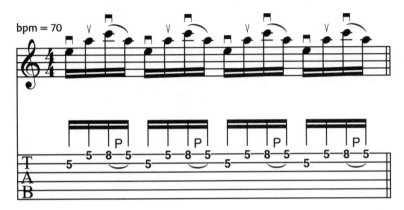

Two-String Lick, Bending the Bottom String Only

Track 143   Use your 3rd finger to bend the bottom note on the 3rd string up a whole step.
The top note on the 2nd string does not get "bent." The two strings should ring
together.

The Ultimate Classic Rock Lick

Track 144   Lay your 1st finger across the 1st and 2nd strings. Bend the 3rd string with your
3rd finger. Start this lick off slowly, then gradually increase the speed.

If you need a review, bends are
covered on pages 57–58.

Variation on the Two-String Bending Lick

Track 145 Use your 3rd or 4th finger to do the pull-off.

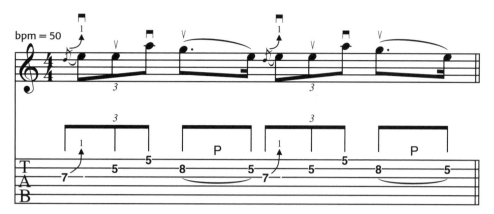

Bending Two Strings at Once

Track 146 For the *double string bend*, put your 4th finger on the 2nd string and 3rd finger on the 3rd string. Hit both strings at the same time and then bend both up a half step and release them quickly. Play the last notes by laying your 1st finger across the two strings at the 5th fret.

The Bend-Friendly C, D, and G Notes of A Minor Pentatonic

Track 147 Review the octave patterns in A (page 85.) G is two frets below A, while C, and D are three and five frets above A. These three notes are particularly good for bending.

Lick in the Style of Jimmy Page

This lick is inspired by Jimmy Page's solo in "Stairway to Heaven." Lots of pull-offs! For the first chord, hit all three strings and immediately bend the 3rd string up a whole step to match the pitch of the 2nd string.

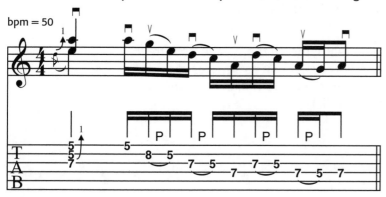

CHORDS THAT SOUND GOOD WITH THE A MINOR PENTATONIC SCALE

- A, D, and E. The I–IV–V chords in the key of A (pages 33, 42, E-shaped barre, 44, A-shaped barre).

- A5, D5, and E5. The I–IV–V chords in the key of A (page 18).

- A7, D7, and E7. The bluesier I–IV–V chords in A (pages 42, 44).

- A9, D9, and E9. The funkier I–IV–V chords in A (page 75). Dominant 7th chords can be replaced by 9th chords in many blues, blues-rock, and soul songs.

- A7, D7, and the "Jimi Hendrix chord" E7(♯9) (page 76).

- A5, C5, D5, E5, and G5. The notes of the A Minor pentatonic scale turned into power chords.

- A7, C7, D7, E7, and G7. The notes of the A Minor pentatonic scale turned into dominant 7th chords. This chord combination sounds like 1960s and '70s classic rock, but blues-influenced indie bands like The Black Keys use these too.

- A7(♯9) when it's the main chord of the song (the I chord).

- Am, Dm, and Em

- Am7, Dm7, and Em7. Minor 7th chords sound less dark and sometimes "jazzier" than regular minor chords (page 74).

You can mix any of the chords on this list, or any chord from the key of C (page 87), as long as the A or Am chord is the main chord.

> **Quick Tip**
>
> You'll find five jam tracks in different rock styles starting on page 77 you can use to practice soloing.
>
> You can also record yourself playing any of the chord combinations listed above. Try using any of the strum patterns on pages 48–51, and play each chord for one or two bars.
>
> Another option is to play the chords of a 12-bar blues (page 55). Just make sure you play A7, D7, and E7 (I–IV–V chords in the key of A).

Pattern 4 on Frets 7–10 (Starts From C): Bringing More Intensity

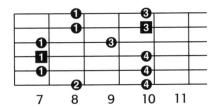

The fourth pattern starts from the note C. It includes many great licks with lots of string bends. It also gives you some higher notes for building more intensity in your solos.

As with any scale you learn, locate the octave pattern within the scale (the two A's shown as squares for this A minor pentatonic scale pattern), run the scale up and down (to make your fingers stronger and learn where the notes are), and then play the licks.

Exercise: Sliding and Bending

Track 149   Use your 3rd finger for the slide and the bend. To control the bend, use your 1st and 2nd fingers to support the 3rd finger.

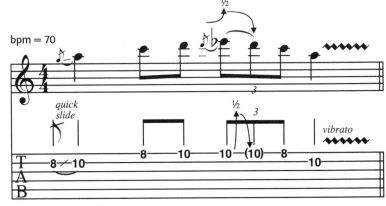

Pre-Bends

In a pre-bend (↑), the note is bent before striking the string. Hit it and then release the bend, but keep your fingers pressed against the string so that you hear the note coming down. It will take some practice and experimentation to know how much to bend the note before hitting the string.

Pre-Bend Lick

Track 150

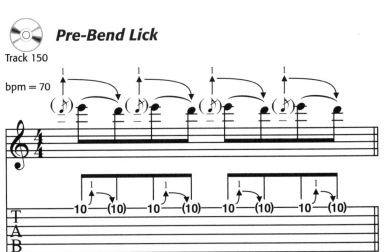

Two Ways to Play a Note

Track 151   Play the fourth note on the 10th fret with your 3rd finger, and then use your 1st finger to play the quick slide from the 8th fret up to the 10th fret. This is a blues-guitar influenced gesture, showing how one note can be made to sound different by changing the technique.

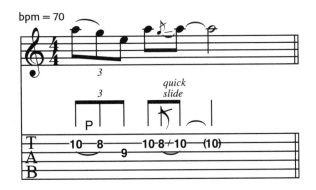

Now let's play some licks that combine patterns 3 and 4. You're gonna like this!

Combining Patterns 3 and 4 in Solos

Try combining the licks from patterns 3 and 4. Here are some ideas.

 Combination Lick No. 1

Track 152
Shuffle—bpm = 70

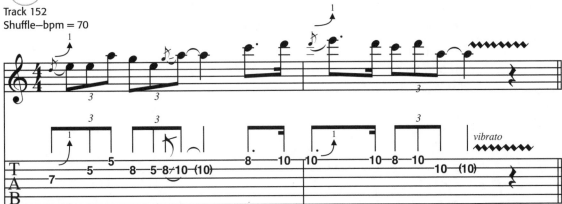

 Combination Lick No. 2

Track 153 Start with your 3rd and 4th fingers doing a two-string bend, similar to Bending Two Strings at Once on page 100. Use your 1st finger to barre the notes at the 5th fret, and your 3rd finger for the slide.

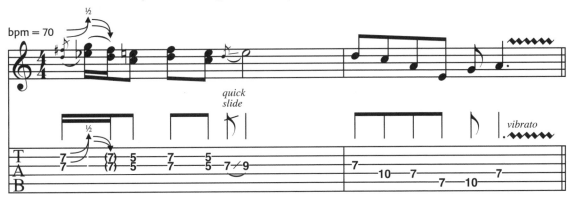

 "Play Like a Pro" tip sections are directed toward more experienced guitar players. If you're new to soloing, skip these for now. It's important that you aren't bound by too many music rules! Just have fun playing the licks.

 ### Play Fills When the Singer Is Quiet

As a guitarist, your role is often to play *fills*—short melodies—in some of the spots where the singer isn't singing. This raises the intensity of the song. Fills can also reflect the singer's emotions and what they're singing about. Usually you get to play more fills as the song progresses (from the second verse and onward).

Your fills should be very short and not detract from the song. Listen to records of all styles and pay attention to what the guitarist plays when the singer is quiet. The licks you've just learned work great as fills. Try creating your own versions of the licks and record them so you don't forget them!

Pattern 5 on Frets 9–13: Making Your Guitar Wail

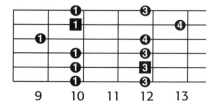

The fifth pattern starts from the note D. Its high notes are great for wailing guitar licks at the peak of a solo. Sometimes as a solo progresses, playing higher and higher notes build drama and intensity.

You can use your 3rd finger to play the 4th-finger notes in some cases, as it's easier to bend strings with your 3rd finger.

Bends and Pull-Offs

Track 154

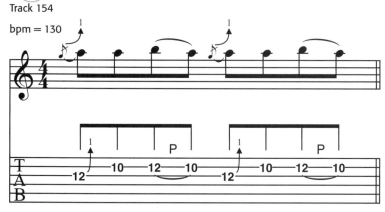

Playing Trills

Track 155 A trill is a very quick succession of hammer-ons and pull-offs. It's best to use your 3rd finger to play the bend and the trill in this example.

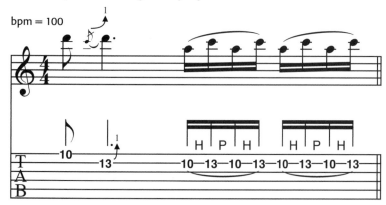

Classic Blues Lick

Track 156 Use your 1st finger for the first note, your 2nd finger for the very subtle and slightly eerie quarter-step bend, and your 1st finger again for the third and last note.

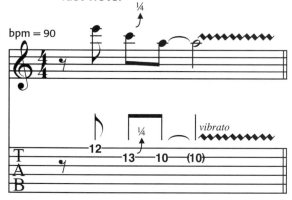

Two Bends, One After Another

Track 157 This one requires good control and finger strength, since you're going to play two string bends in a row. Use three fingers to do the bends, and have fun!

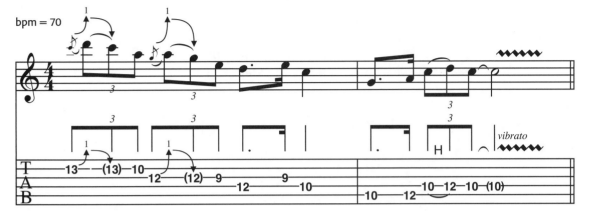

Pull-Offs and Slides

Track 158 Use your 3rd finger for the pull-offs and the note on 4th string at the 12th fret. Play the quick slide with your 1st finger.

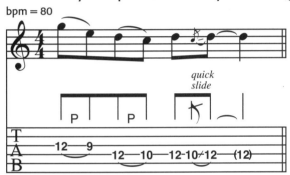

Use Different Lengths of Notes

When soloing, remember to vary the rhythm. Play notes of different lengths. Think of solos as being like talking; mix short and long sentences, take a breath, be silent for a moment.

Try this experiment. You'll be surprised at how different you'll sound!

1. Record yourself playing freely over some chords, then put the recording device away.

2. Only improvise with long notes. Play whole notes (four beats each) until you run out of ideas.

3. Improvise the same way with just quarter notes (one beat each).

4. If you can, play in a steady stream of eighth notes (two notes for each beat).

5. Now bring your recording device out again. Start improvising freely, varying the lengths of the notes.

Compare your first and second recording. It is very likely your soloing sounded more varied and interesting the second time.

There are other kinds of eighth and sixteenth note rhythms that are well worth exploring: ♫, ♫, ♫, and ♫, for example. They'll give your solos a lot more groove!

Pattern 1 Again on Frets 12–15: Over the Top

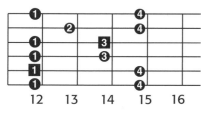

You've come full circle. You've played the five patterns of A minor pentatonic, each one starting on a different note in the scale. There are many fantastic rock licks, however, that come from pattern 1 if you take it up an octave. Start it at the 12th fret this time. Here are some really expressive licks for the peak of a solo.

Bend and Release

Track 159 Release the bend in the first bar slowly. In the second bar, release quickly. Use your 3rd finger for both.

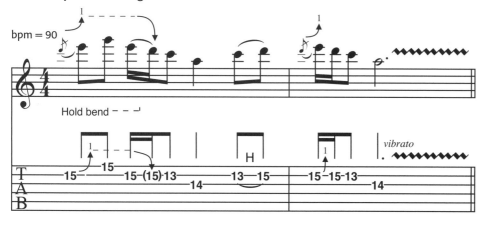

Bend and Trill

Track 160 Play the bend with your 3rd finger. You can do the trill with either your 3rd or 4th finger.

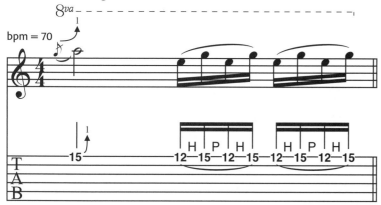

Gradually Released Bend

Track 161 Jimi Hendrix is one of many guitarists who have used this technique. Bend the string and gradually release it, little-by-little. The note sounds like it's crashing down.

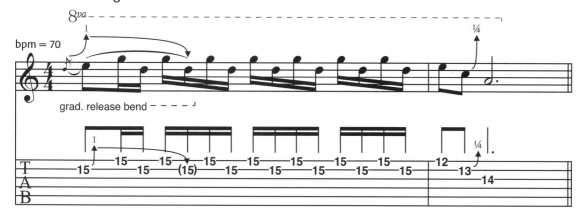

Famous Rock Songs for Your Minor Pentatonic Soloing Practice

"Black Dog," "Rock and Roll"... Led Zeppelin (key of A)

"Problem Child," "Whole Lotta Rosie"..................................... AC/DC (key of A)

"While My Guitar Gently Weeps" (Am section/guitar solo)............ The Beatles (key of A minor)

"Dead Leaves and the Dirty Ground"....................................... The White Stripes (key of A)

"Smoke on the Water".. Deep Purple (key of G: pattern 3 starts at 3rd fret)

"Gold on the Ceiling"... The Black Keys (key of G)

"You Ain't Alone"... Alabama Shakes (key of C, pattern 3 at 8th fret)

"Fall Behind Me".. The Donnas (key of D, pattern 3 at 10th fret)

"Purple Haze".. Jimi Hendrix (key of E, pattern 3 at 12th fret)

"Frozen".. Orianthi (key of E)

"Paris (Ooh La La)".. Grace Potter & The Nocturnals (key of F♯, pattern 3 at 2nd fret)

Songs by Female Blues Guitarists

"Come on in My Kitchen".. Rory Block (key of B♭: pattern 3 starts at 6th fret)

"Business as Usual".. Ana Popovic (key of D)

"Finest Lovin' Man".. Bonnie Raitt (key of E)

"Roll with Me".. Deborah Coleman (key of E)

"Rock Me Right".. Susan Tedeschi (key of E)

"Me and My Chauffeur Blues"... Memphis Minnie (key of G)

"Down the Big Road Blues".. Sue Foley (key of G)

Don't forget that you can solo over the five jam tracks starting on page 77, too!

"Recordings that I jammed along to? Santana's (concert DVD) Sacred Fire: Live in Mexico *was my favorite. Carlos' playing is so inspiring; his soloing is very colorful here."*

Orianthi Panagaris, *guitarist, singer and songwriter (Michael Jackson, Alice Cooper, solo artist)*

HOW TO BUILD A SOLO

There are two types of guitar solos: *improvised* (making things up as you go), and *composed* (planning it out, and even writing it down, beforehand). You can hear the second category in "Hotel California," "Sweet Child o' Mine," or "Stairway to Heaven." They're like songs within the songs. It's best to be able to play both types of solos.

Here are some tips on how to build a great solo:

- Don't fire off your most interesting ideas right at the beginning because then you'll have nowhere else to go. Start simply, even revisiting the same phrase over several different chords.

- Variety is good! Try to shift between lower, midrange, and higher notes as you go. Use dynamics (loud and soft). Include moments of silence. Vary your rhythmic phrasing, playing notes of different lengths. These things will give your solos more impact.

- Save the highest, most wailing notes for the end. You can even play a very repetitive lick. If you play it with lots of passion and your band backs you up, it'll sound good.

PUTTING IT ALL TOGETHER—12-BAR BLUESY ROCK SOLO IN A MINOR

Track 162

Learning some blues guitar is important for anyone who wants to be a better rock lead guitarist. You'll learn the coolest licks, how to play over chord changes, and how to use groove and silence. Soloing over a 12-bar blues helps you learn how to know where you are in the song, and there are so many great female blues guitarists today to inspire you: Bonnie Raitt, Debbie Davies, and Susan Tedeschi to name just a very few.

In this 12-bar solo, you'll use all the A minor pentatonic patterns and the concepts mentioned earlier. You'll play lots of bends and slides. Listen to the track multiple times, and practice the solo very slowly, lick by lick. Have fun with it!

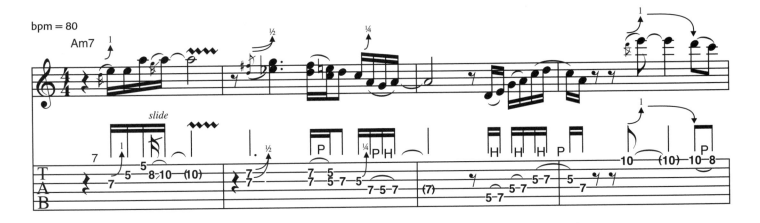

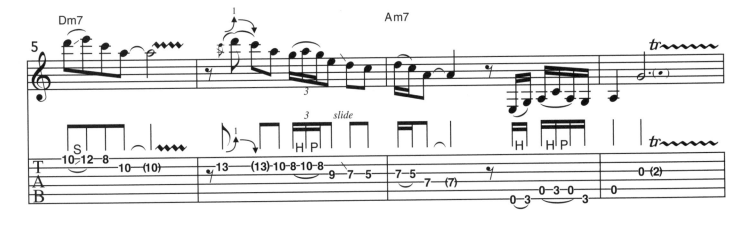

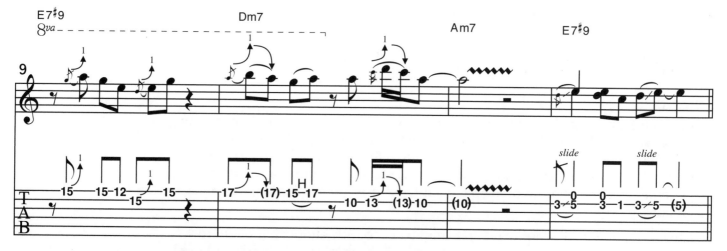

Wrapping Up: The Sliding Minor Pentatonic Scale in A

In addition to the five patterns of the A minor pentatonic scale, there's also a version that lets you slide across the fretboard. You don't have to slide into notes, but it's fun to do, so let's try it out!

NOTE: In this pattern, all of the root notes (A) are played with your 3rd finger.

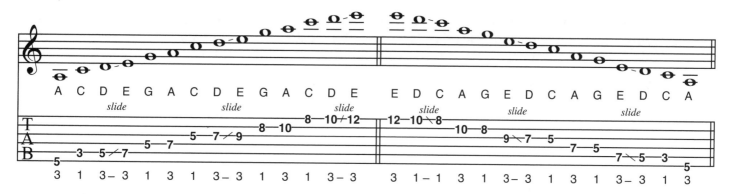

Here's another way you can play this scale by starting on A at the 5th string, 12th fret.

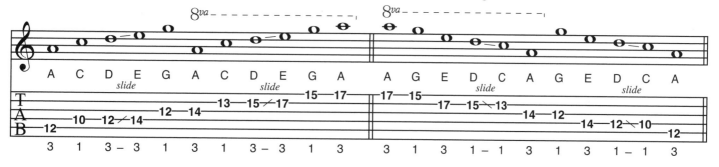

Combining Sliding Scale and Pattern 3 Lick

Track 163 — Start the lick with your 3rd finger. Barre the 2nd and 3rd strings at the 5th fret with your 1st finger, and bend them a quarter step up by pulling the strings down just a bit.

bpm = 110

Congratulations for having come this far! Now, let's explore more advanced techniques, such as tapping, tremolo picking, pinched harmonics, and how to use the whammy bar.

MORE ADVANCED ROCK TECHNIQUES

Following is a very brief introduction to some of the techniques you may have noticed when thumbing through guitar magazines.

Legato

As you learned on page 56, legato is a smooth, connected sound created by sounding the notes with the fretting hand, without picking the strings. These techniques, such as hammer-ons and pull-offs, can create fast runs with a rolling, fluid sound. Legato playing is easiest when playing notes that are close together on the same string, since it takes some time and effort to develop the left-hand strength required for lots of legato techniques.

Legato is common in all styles of playing, from blues to rock, although modern rock guitarists and technical guitar virtuosos ("shredders") have taken it to a different level. One song that is a great legato showcase is Joe Satriani's "Flying In a Blue Dream." Orianthi also plays legato phrases in her solo on "According to You."

In music and tablature, legato is indicated with a *slur*, which is a curved line connecting two or more notes.

C Major Scale—Legato Run and Lick

Track 164   Memorizing your scale patterns is important for legato playing. They are often strung together to create long licks. Let's try a shorter legato run on a C major scale (pattern 4 from page 88). Be sure to use the suggested fingerings. After the scale, you'll play a lick that uses the scale notes, so you can see how this technique can be used for melodies.

NOTE: Each string is picked only once. The rest of the scale notes are played with hammer-ons. The lick in the last bar is played with hammer-ons and pull-offs.

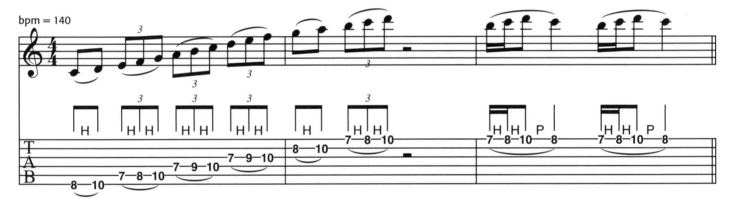

A Minor Pentatonic Scale—Legato Run and Lick

Track 165   Legato licks that are built on a scale run are very common in rock lead guitar. Try this lick based on pattern 3 of the A minor pentatonic scale. Play it slowly at first.

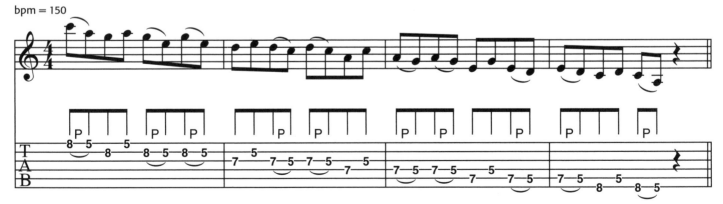

Two-Handed Tapping

In *two-handed tapping*, hammer-ons and pull-offs are used in a different way. Your picking hand taps the strings against the fretboard, while the fingers of your fretting hand play a sequence of notes in sync with your tapping hand (see photo on right).

Tapping allows you to easily play multiple notes in fast succession. Eddie Van Halen and Jennifer Batten are masters of tapping, and Batten even wrote a book on the subject, *Two Hand Rock*. Marnie Stern is an indie rock artist who uses tapping a lot in her songwriting.

When you're new at tapping, you may get blisters on your fingertips because you're hitting them against metal strings. Over time, you will build up protective calluses.

In music and tablature, a note that is played with your tapping hand is indicated with a capital "T."

Track 166

Tapping in the Style of Orianthi's "According to You"

Orianthi plays in an alternate tuning on her recording, and the tapping in her solo is done very fast. She basically plays around the first three notes of a B♭ major scale, then a C major scale, and then a D natural minor scale, letting the peak of her solo mirror the song's ascending power chords: B♭5, C5, and D5. This example in standard tuning is slowed down so that you can more easily hear how the tapping is done.

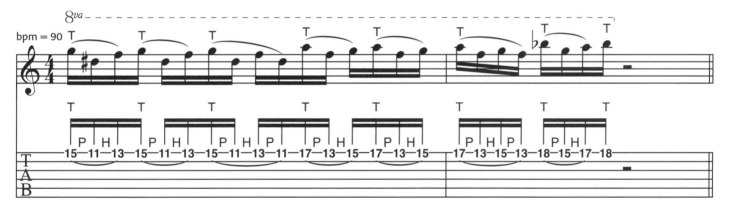

"Conditioning the fingers is the same process for right hand tapping as it is for the left hand fretting. You need to play regularly and consistently to maintain tough finger tips. It's probably best to limit the time you put in at first so you stop before they feel tender. You can even start with lighter strings and low action *and build it up. The calluses will grow pretty quickly."*

***Jennifer Batten**, guitarist and composer (Michael Jackson, Jeff Beck, solo artist)*

Action refers to the distance between the strings and the fretboard. *Low action* means that the strings are close to the fretboard.

Photo by Brent J. Angelo

The Whammy Bar

Bigsby tremolo

Fender trem arm

Floyd Rose system

Whammy bar, *trem arm*, *vibrato bar*, etc., are all devices which enable you to loosen or tighten the strings, creating anything from a subtle vibrato to intense pitch-bend effects. In TAB, this is indicated by a wavy line with the text "w/Bar."

Jimi Hendrix was one of the first to use it famously in his live version of "The Star Spangled Banner." Jeff Beck, Steve Vai, and indie bands like Sonic Youth use it, too.

The Bigbsy and Fender tremolos allow a light vibrato, but easily go out of tune if you push them too hard. The Floyd Rose system allows players to go for extreme effects and still maintain tuning stability.

Using a Whammy Bar at the End of a Lick

Track 167 Let's end this C major scale lick by pushing your whammy bar down lightly twice.

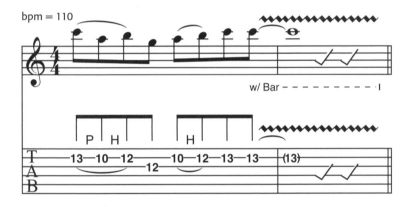

> ✓ = *Whammy bar dip.* Push down lightly on the whammy bar.

Tremolo Picking

In *tremolo picking*, the tip of your pick or the fingers are used to rapidly repeat a single note very quickly and evenly. This can be heard in Eddie Van Halen's "Eruption." In TAB, tremolo picking is indicated with three slashes (≋).

Tremolo in the style of Muse on "Blackout"

Track 168 The more relaxed your hand and arm are, the better your tremolo picking will sound!

> **Tremolo**
> This is a tremolo sign.
> ≋
> For guitarists, it means to rapidly repeat a single note to create the impression of sustain.

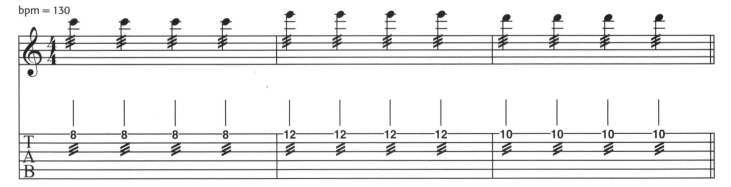

Natural Harmonics

Harmonics are very clear, pure tones. To create the bell-like sound of a harmonic, touch the string very lightly directly above certain frets. These harmonics are called *natural harmonics* because they occur naturally at certain divisions of a string's length. Natural harmonics can be played on all strings at many frets, but they are easiest to find and produce at the 12th, 7th, 5th, and 9th frets.

In TAB, harmonics are indicated by a diamond shape (◇) above the note. In standard music notation, the notes themselves have a diamond shape.

Melody with Natural Harmonics
Track 169

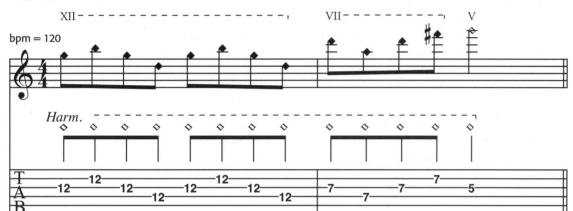

Pinched Harmonics

Roy Buchanan popularized the *pinched harmonic* technique, where the thumb of your picking hand catches the string very slightly right after picking the note. This "double attack" of thumb and pick creates an *artificial harmonic*, which has a high squealing effect. Billy Gibbons from ZZ Top uses this a lot, and Zakk Wylde has made it his trademark. Metal guitarists often combine pinched harmonics with the whammy bar and loud amp distortion to get the most extreme sounds. In TAB, pinched harmonics are indicated by the letters "PH".

Pinched Harmonics in the Style of ZZ Top's "La Grange"
Track 170 Hold most of the pick between your thumb and index finger so that your thumb stays close to the string. Practice slowly with just one or two notes, making sure your thumb is creating the pinched harmonic effect. The notes are struck with the very tip of the pick.

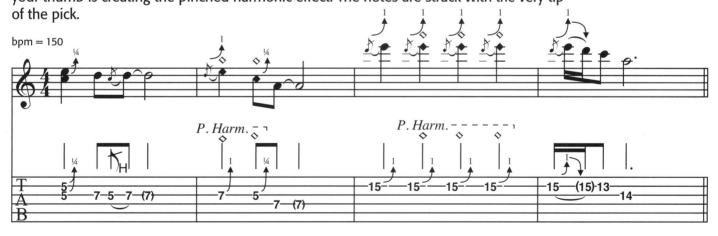

Pick some chords and create a tasty 4-bar solo. Next, try 8-, 12-, and 24-bar solos. Don't feel like you have write epic stuff; just have fun!

You've completed the Lead Guitar Section! Great job! Now it's time to dig into some basics about rock songs, and how to write a song chart for your band.

Section 4: All About the Song

You can play all sorts of fancy chords and have the fiercest lead guitar chops in the world, but it all needs to serve the song you're playing. Let's take a look at the most popular song structures in rock, what the different sections within a song do, and how to write a song chart. This will help you figure out a cover song, or show your band mates one of your new songs.

THE MOST POPULAR SONG STRUCTURES IN ROCK

If you want to cover a song and learn it as quickly as possible, figure out what structure it has before you learn the chords, melody, and lyrics. Most rock songs follow a set structure for how the different sections unfold. The three most common song structures (or song forms) in rock are the 12-bar blues, verse/chorus, and AABA. Let's take a closer look at each of them.

12-Bar Blues

A standard 12-bar blues song is a I–IV–V progression with three lyric phrases. Each phrase is four bars long. Phrase 1 is sung over the I chord on bars 1–4. Phrase 2 repeats the lyrics from Phrase 1 and is sung over the IV chord on bars 5–8. After the singer sings a phrase, there's a space left where a guitarist or other instrumentalist can respond with a solo lick. This interaction is called *call and response*.

Phrase 3 goes from the V chord to the IV chord, and then the last two bars create something called the *turnaround* (see page 55). Lyrically, Phrase 3 is like a punch line or response to what was sung in the first two phrases.

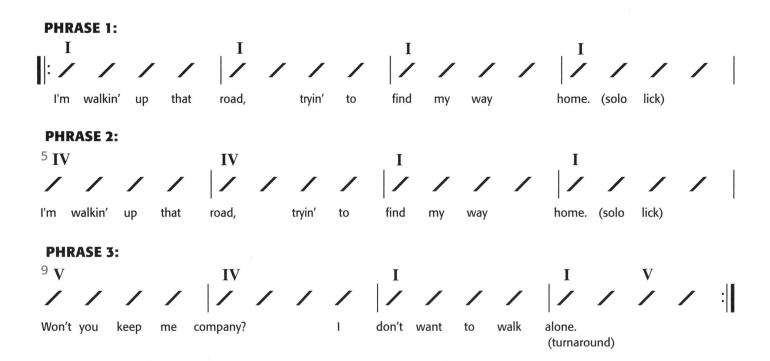

NOTE: The slash symbols (/)tell you to strum a chord for four beats in each bar.

Verse/Chorus Songs

This is the most common structure for rock songs by far. It also tends to have more sections, so let's talk about the structure.

The *verses* gradually unfold the story and characters— the who, where, and when. Sometimes (not always), the verses are followed by a *pre-chorus* with different chords. Musically and lyrically, the pre-chorus serves to build up excitement and make us want to hear the *chorus*, which carries the message of the song. This is where you usually find the title of the song.

After repeating these sections, there is often a *bridge*, which can have a completely different rhythmic feel, melody, chord changes, and lyric content. The purpose of the bridge is to give our ears a break after all the repeated sections. In rock songs, there is often a guitar solo following the bridge. All of this delaying serves to make us want to hear the chorus again and again until the song ends.

In addition, many songs have an *intro* (usually instrumental) to lure the listener in, and sometimes also an *outro* (also called *coda* or *tag*) at the very end.

VERSE 1:

/ / / / | / / / / | / / / / | / / / / | / / / / | / / / / | / / / / | / / / / |

PRE-CHORUS:

/ / / / | / / / / | / / / / | / / / / |

CHORUS:

/ / / / | / / / / | / / / / | / / / / | / / / / | / / / / | / / / / | / / / / |

VERSE 2 (OR 3):

/ / / / | / / / / | / / / / | / / / / | / / / / | / / / / | / / / / | / / / / |

PRE-CHORUS: (or skip it and go straight to the chorus)

/ / / / | / / / / | / / / / | / / / / |

CHORUS:

/ / / / | / / / / | / / / / | / / / / | / / / / | / / / / | / / / / | / / / / |

BRIDGE: (Sometimes called the "middle eight." Sometimes followed by a guitar solo.)

/ / / / | / / / / | / / / / | / / / / | / / / / | / / / / |

FINAL CHORUS: (Sometimes repeated)

/ / / / | / / / / | / / / / | / / / / | / / / / | / / / / ‖

Many verses and choruses are four, eight, or sixteen bars each. This rule isn't set in stone, though. If you have a lyric that needs a nine-bar verse, go ahead!

AABA Songs

You hear this song form in many Beatles songs like "Yesterday," and also in jazz standards and songs from musicals (Broadway). It isn't as common in rock and pop today, but it's still used, and there are too many legendary rock songs that are written in the AABA form for it to be ignored. Here's a typical example of the AABA form:

A: (The main theme)

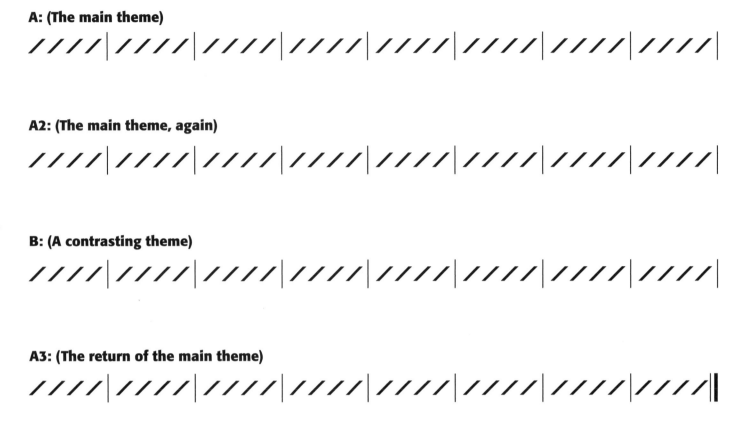

A2: (The main theme, again)

B: (A contrasting theme)

A3: (The return of the main theme)

In these types of songs, the title is often found in the A sections. That's one reason why you don't refer to their B section as the chorus.

How to Write a Chord Chart for a Song

Chart is musical slang for the word *score*, which refers to the organized notation of a piece or song. Try to write your chart on just one page. Use a blank piece of paper. Write with clear block letters so that your band mates can read it while playing.

1. Split the song up into its different sections: intro, verse, etc. If you have two verses with the same chords, you only need to write one verse. Above it, write "Verse 1 and 2." Write repeat signs at the start and the end of the section if it does repeat (make sure your band mates know what the signs mean).

2. Figure out how many bars there are in each section. After each bar, draw a horizontal dash. These will be your bar lines (see page 16).

3. Write the chord changes for each section. If you have two bars of the same chord, just write the chord name in the first bar. If there are more than one chord in a bar, write the multiple chords between the bar lines. Draw slash symbols above or below the chords to show how many beats each one gets, like the 12-bar blues on page 114.

Take a look at the verse/chorus song chart on the next page!

Here's a basic chord chart for one of my band's songs. Always tell your fellow musicians the time signature and tempo of the song. This tune is in $\frac{4}{4}$ time, and the tempo is 80 bpm (beats per minute).

Don't write the chords of the sections directly underneath each other, as it's easy to mix them up that way.

SAY WHAT YOU THINK

(THE NIKKI O'NEILL BAND)

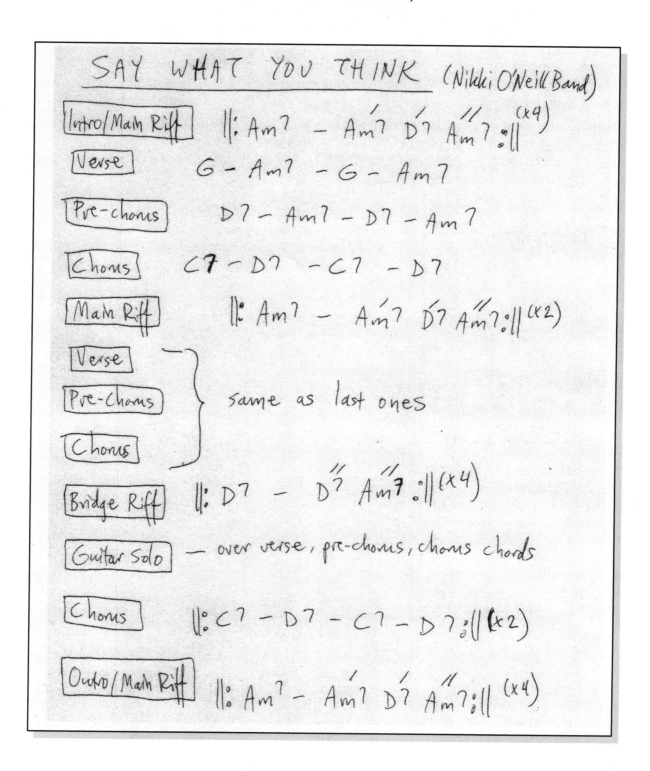

Section 5: Amps, Effects and Guitar Care

In this section, you'll learn the basics about amplifiers (amps) designed for the electric guitar, what different effects do, and some simple ways to care for your guitar.

UNDERSTAND YOUR AMP

Let's go over the three most common amplifier types, the controls of the front panel, the basic parts inside an amp (including tubes), and define and discuss distortion.

Tube Amps, Solid State, and Digital Amps

All guitar amps have two basic components: the *head* (the electronics that comprise the amplifier) and the speakers. A *combo amp* is one where the head and speaker cabinet are together in a single unit. It is also possible for the head and cabinet to be separate. Combos tend to have one or two speakers, while cabinets can have more. The term "4x12," for instance, means that there are four speakers and that each one is 12 inches wide in diameter.

Wattage is the power rating of the amp. A small practice amp has a very low wattage. If you plan on rehearsing and playing small to medium clubs with a band (especially with a drummer), you need a 10–30W tube amp or a 30–50W solid-state amp. Amps with more wattage are needed for large venues.

Tube amps are favored by guitarists who prefer a warmer classic rock sound with a distortion that is rich in harmonic overtones. What shapes their sound is a number of *vacuum tubes*. When you turn on a tube amp, it takes a moment before you hear your guitar, because the tubes need to get up and running. These amps are often heavier and louder than other amp types.

Solid-state amps don't have tubes. Instead, their sound mainly comes from transistors or integrated circuits and microchips. Fans of tube amps think solid state amps sound clinical, but many contemporary metal guitarists (like Dimebag Darrell) swear by them as they can get a very "tight" distortion sound, which works perfectly for *de-tuned* (some metal bands tune their guitars lower, for a heavier sound), brutal metal riffing.

Digital amps came out in the 1990s. They digitally replicate the sounds of famous amps and also include some effects. Some critics think they sound "fake." But in recording studios, software versions of these amps (called *amp modelers*) are popular among many sound engineers, as they can easily enhance already recorded guitar tones.

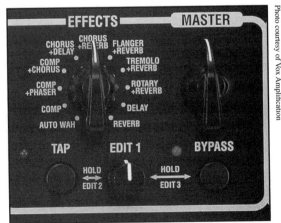

Effects selector on Vox DA15 modeling amp.

The Front Panel

This is a typical front panel on a guitar amp. Here is where you dial in your sound!

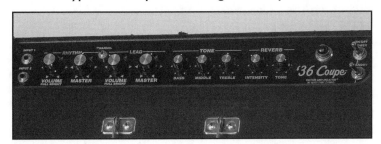

Your guitar is plugged into an input jack. Some amps have an extra input designed to give you a lower volume and cleaner sound if you use effects.

On many amps there are separate volume controls for rhythm guitar and louder lead guitar sounds. A footswitch is used to easily alternate between the two (the footswitch is plugged to the back of the amp). The master volume is the main volume, while the regular volume (also called *gain*) adjusts the amount of distortion. For a cleaner sound, use less gain and more master volume. For heavier distortion, turn up the gain instead and lower the master volume. Some amps also have a *pull bright* function; if you pull the gain knob outward, you get a brighter sound.

Usually amps have a few tone controls like bass, middle, and treble (it might say "EQ" or "Equalizer" above these knobs). When playing very loud, it is a good idea to lower the bass and create a tighter, less booming sound. Metal guitarists tend to turn down the middle ("mid"). Treble increases the high frequencies.

Reverb creates the effect of playing in a large room. Not all amps have reverb. If there's a reverb tone knob, you can create different kinds of reverb from bright to warm. The amount of reverb in your sound is controlled with the *intensity* knob.

Footswitch and back panel.

Inside a Tube Amp

WARNING! Never poke around inside an amp on your own. There are certain parts of the amp that can store a deadly charge, even if you've had the amp turned off for several days. So always let a professional (who regularly works with all kinds of amps) change parts or do any kind of repairs on it.

Blackheart single-ended Class A amp chassis

The Tubes

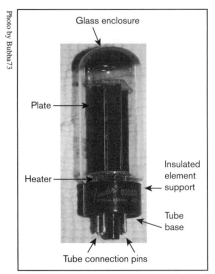

Glass enclosure

Plate

Heater

Insulated element support

Tube base

Tube connection pins

Vacuum tube with parts labeled.

Tubes—or valves, as they're called in the U.K.—used to exist in all kinds of electronics like radios and TV sets, but now you'll only find them in certain high-end microphones, studio equipment, and guitar amps. Most tubes are made in a few factories in Eastern Europe and China. Many guitarists love tubes because they create a distorted amp sound that sounds warm and rich with a slightly unpredictable delivery that's part of the "magic."

Tubes operate in two places inside an amp: the preamp, which is where the guitar tone is shaped, and in the power amp, which generates the volume.

Common preamp tube models are the 12AX7 and 12AU7. The power amp tubes are much larger. Since they take more of a beating because of their location, they need to be replaced more often (how often depends on how much and how loud you play). If the amp sounds duller and quieter, that's your cue. Since they work in tandem, they usually need to be replaced all at once.

There are many different power amp tube models, designed to fit either American or British-style Fender, Marshall, or Mesa Boogie amps (as well as other amps that are designed like these three models). Common tube models are 6L6, EL34, EL84, and 6550. If you have a tube amp, check your manual to see which tubes your amp uses. Stick with the same models and let a pro replace them.

What Is Distortion?

Demonstration of "Crunch" Overdrive and Distortion

Track 171

When we think of the sound of rock guitar, we usually don't think of nice and crystal-clear sounds. The sound we usually imagine—a raunchy and biting sound—comes from what we call *distortion*.

When an amp is turned up, its power amp component (the part that generates the volume) is pushing the speakers, which have a limited frequency range. If it is a tube amp, the power amp tubes also get pushed to the limit. As a result of all this, the guitar tone "breaks up" and creates distortion.

In the 1960s, you had to turn your amp up insanely loud to achieve this effect. Nowadays, amps are built to create distortion on lower volumes, with just the turn of a knob. You can also buy distortion effects pedals (more on that soon).

There are different ranges of distortion. Many players use a bit of "crunch," or just a bit of "dirt," while the most intense amounts of distortion can be heard in hard rock and metal.

A GUIDE TO EFFECTS PEDALS

Effects pedals color your sound in addition to the "dry" sound you get with just a guitar and amp.

You can buy single pedals or multi-effects, which are a combination of several effects. Multi-effects come as pedals, which you control with your foot, or as rack-mountable units with knobs that you dial in (these are better for recording than stage use).

Pedals are easy to use. They have a built-in footswitch, so that you can turn the effect on and off with the tap of your foot. That's why they're also called *stomp boxes*. Multi-effects are programmable and give you the ability to use several sound effects simultaneously.

If your budget is tight or you don't know which pedals to try first, start with a good delay and a wah. A great amp will give great-sounding distortion. If you don't like the sound of your amp's distortion or you need more of it, get a distortion pedal.

Rocktron's HUSH pedal

Overdrive, Distortion, and Fuzz

Boss's Distortion Pedal.

 Demonstrating Overdrive, Dist, Fuzz

Track 172   The powerful *overdriven* amplifier sound—which happens when an amp is overpowered with sheer volume—is one of the most sought-after sounds by guitarists. Overdrive makes your tone sound "broken," but in the right way! You can get all kinds of flavors, from amp-like overdrive pedals to the more intense distortion pedals, or the really extreme "dists" for metal sounds.

Fuzz tones fall somewhere between overdrive and distortion. This effect came out in the 1960s and was used especially by Jimi Hendrix. Not everybody likes it; fuzz has a stinging, in-your-face quality, but it's a must for psychedelic rock.

Wah and Envelope Filter (Auto Wah)

The *wah pedal* is probably the most popular guitar effect besides distortion. Say the word and you'll hear what it sounds like! Or listen to the intro to Jimi Hendrix's "Voodoo Child" and funky disco tunes, like "Car Wash." Sly Stone connected it to his vocal mic as he sang his classic anti-racism song "Don't Call Me Ni**er (Whitey)."

It's a foot-controlled tone potentiometer ("tone pot") similar to the tone control knobs you have on your electric guitar. By moving the pedal up and down with your foot, you shift the tonal balance.

Envelope Filters (also called *Envelope Followers*, *Dynamic Filters*, *Auto Wah*, or *Touch Wah*) allow wah-styled effects without using a foot control. Once the pedal is on, it automatically produces a sweeping wah-like effect. This effect usually responds to the picking *attack* as well (how hard or soft you hit the strings). They can't replace a real wah pedal, but a lot of funk and rock guitarists and bass players use them.

Demonstration of Wah and Envelope Filter

Track 173

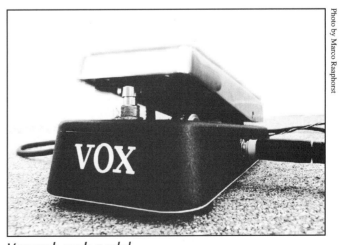

Vox wah-wah pedal

Equalizer

Demonstration of Equalizer

Track 174   An *equalizer*, or *EQ*, is a tone control with which you can shape the *timbre* (color or character) of the sound in different frequencies: low, mid, and high range. It's usually a feature on amps, but it's great if you want to create even more tonal variety, or if you want to accentuate or get rid of unwanted frequencies in your amp or guitar tone. The most common EQ types are *graphic* (the simplest type, consists of multiple sliders or controls for boosting or cutting bands or frequencies of sound) and *parametric* (a more complex type, which controls more parameters of the sound).

Professional sound analog equalization rack with UREI graphic and parametric EQs

Reverb and Delay

Reverb simulates acoustic room sounds. Singers usually like to have some reverb added to their vocals. Most guitar amplifiers have built-in reverb, but you can buy really sophisticated rack units for studio use. They offer more control and variables like room size (room, hall, cathedral).

Delay is a repetitive echo that samples what you play and plays it back to you after a specified amount of time. Listen to The Edge from U2 and you'll hear what it sounds like. You can set the number of repetitions and the time (either by seconds or by bars, beats, and tempo). Modern delays have pretty long loops, allowing you to jam and harmonize guitar parts with yourself!

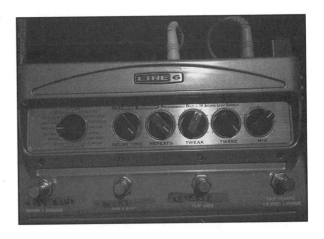

Demonstration of Reverb

Track 175

Demonstration of Delay

Track 176

Modulation Effects: Chorus, Flanger, Phaser, Vibrato, Tremolo and Rotary

Modulation effects get their sound from an *oscillator* (an electronic circuit that produces a repetitive, oscillating electronic signal), which creates a repeating sweep of the effect. You choose the speed of the sweep with a rate control knob.

The *chorus* effect almost creates the sound of a 12-string guitar. It creates a doubling effect: the notes you play get "twin notes" that sweep up and down in the same pitch. Check out records by The Police to hear this; Andy Summers used a Roland Jazz Chorus amp to create his unmistakable sound.

Demonstration of Chorus

Track 177

Photo by Robert Harker/Wikimedia Commons

A *flanger* is related to the chorus, but has a much more metallic sound. Famous song examples include the intro to Heart's "Barracuda" and the middle section of Lenny Kravitz's "Are You Gonna Go My Way."

 Demonstration of Flanger

Track 178

A *phaser* creates a swooshing, gradual sweep. Extremely popular in the 1970s, it was used by singers, drummers, bass players, and guitarists. Hear it on the first Van Halen records or funk tunes, like Parliament's hit "Flash Light."

 Demonstration of Phaser

Track 179

Vibrato was made popular by Jimi Hendrix. The controls resemble those on phase pedals; the intensity knob controls the degree of the effect, and the speed knob controls the rate of vibrato.

 Demonstration of Vibrato

Track 180

Tremolo sounds like someone turning your amp volume up and down as you play. It has a classic 1950s and '60s sound and can be heard in all kinds of music today, from blues to country.

 Demonstration of Tremolo

Track 181

Rotary is a simulation of a *Leslie* organ cabinet. A Leslie is a spinning speaker system that creates a haunting, trembling sound. It's popular in surf music. You can also hear it on Soundgarden's "Black Hole Sun."

 Demonstration of Rotary

Track 182

Dynamic Effects: Compressors, Sustainers and Limiters

Compression reduces or boosts uneven signal levels to create a balanced and even sound. If you hit the strings too hard, it brings the volume down. If you played so soft that it's too quiet in the mix, it raises the volume. This is a standard effect in recording studios for all instruments.

 Demonstration: Playing with and without Compression

Track 183

Sustain emphasizes the weaker signals. When you hit a note and it starts to *decay* (fade), the sustainer gives it an extra push and lets it ring longer. Unfortunately, sustainers also boost all kinds of humming and *white noise* (a random hissing sound).

A *limiter* cuts your volume at a pre-set threshold peak. It doesn't change your tone. It's good to have in studios if amps "cave in" from guitarists' strong string attacks.

Octavers, Pitch Shifters, and Harmonizers

Octaver pedals fatten up your guitar tone by adding a note that's an octave above or below the one you're playing. Some pedals today can stretch the pitch to two octaves and even let you play chords. Jack White often uses octave pedals. Prince's song "Temptation," which also has tons of delay, is a great showcase for the octaver effect.

 Demonstration of Octave Pedal

Track 184

Pitch shifting simulates the dive-bombing sound of a guitar's Floyd Rose whammy bar. It can also expand your overall note range and produce pitch bends and harmony shifts. A pitch shifter usually has a foot pedal, like a wah. Tom Morello from Rage Against the Machine made this effect famous. He was able to make his guitar sound like a hip-hop DJ's scratching turntable.

Harmonizers have been embraced by guitar wizards like Steve Vai, Orianthi, and Brian May. Unlike the octaver, they can create additional *intervals* (an interval is the distance between two notes), such as 4ths and 5ths. Intelligent pitch shifters create harmony by detecting the pitch you're playing and incorporating the appropriate interval structure. Conventional pitch shifting just performs the interval you set, whether it sounds good or bad with what you're playing. Rack-mounted harmonizers can be pricey.

 Demonstration of Harmonizer

Track 185

Noise Reduction

Noise gates help you quiet all the hissing sounds from amps, long chains of effects pedals, long connecting patch cables, single-coil guitar pickups, and fluorescent lights!

Oddball Effects: Talk Boxes and Acoustic Simulators

Talk boxes were really hip in the early 1970s. You'll hear it on Peter Frampton's "Do You Feel Like I Do?" and Bon Jovi's "Living on a Prayer." A talk box has a long plastic tube that is held in your mouth. Your mic goes through a PA system, like normal. When you talk or sing, the sound travels to the effects box and your tone is manipulated by changing the shape of your mouth.

Acoustic simulators change the tonal spectrum and EQ of your electric guitar so that it sounds like a plugged-in, thin-bodied, acoustic guitar.

 Demonstration of Acoustic Simulator

Track 186

Finally: How to Combine Your Effects

Tons of pedals can get quite noisy. Try to get the best possible amp sound before you add pedals. Here are some common setups from guitar to amp that you can use as a reference:

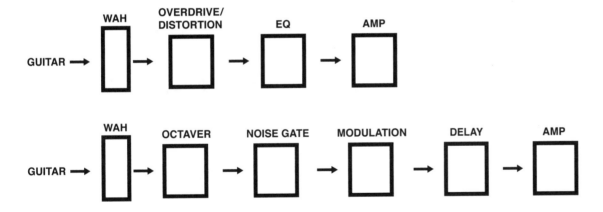

DO NOT:

- Put overdrive at the end of the chain. All your effects will sound distorted. Ugh!
- Place reverb before the other effects. This adds reverb to all the other effects!

Pedalboards are great for keeping many effects organized. They often have 9-Volt outlets (you don't want stompbox batteries dying on you at a show). Right-angled ¼-inch cables are great for connecting pedals to each other. Better brands are worth the expense, as they reduce noise (but they don't need to be the priciest).

Following are some cheap and easy ways that you can maintain your guitar.

Polish Your Body

A flannelette

Grab a guitar polishing cloth (one of those beige chamois cloths, or *flannelettes*, you see at guitar stores). Breathe on your guitar and polish vigorously. This gets rid of fingerprints and sweat. *Never use house-cleaning chemicals on a guitar!* You can buy guitar polish at a music store if you feel you must.

How to Get Rid of Old Stickers

That's a tough one! Don't peel the sticker. Get a small, lint-free cloth. Put a little *naphtha* or lighter fluid (which contains naphtha) on it. Rub the sticker with the cloth. Note: naphtha is highly flammable, so keep it away from candles and other sources of fire. If there's any residue afterwards, buff it out with a clean cloth and some guitar polish.

Pamper Your Fretboard (When the Strings Are Off)

Maple fretboards (light-colored wood) already have a protective finish, so you just need to polish them with a little guitar polish. Remove the strings to do this. For rosewood and ebony fretboards, buy a little bottle of lemon oil from a guitar store. Put a few drops of it onto the fretboard and spread it out evenly with an old, used toothbrush. Let it soak for five minutes, and then wipe off any excess oil. Put on new strings afterwards.

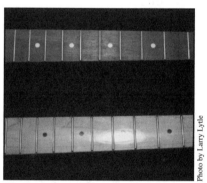

Notice the different finishes on the lighter, maple neck and the darker, rosewood.

Creaking Sounds During Tuning

If you hear a creaking sound when you're tuning, it's because the string is stuck in the nut slot. Mash up a bit of graphite from a pencil together with a tiny bit of petroleum jelly, grab a toothpick, and, with the strings removed, use this mixture to lubricate the string slots. You can also go to a luthier and replace the nut on your guitar with a graphite nut.

If you don't know how to change strings on your electric guitar, worry not–there are many great videos online that teach you how to do that. You can also check out *Teach Yourself Guitar Repair and Maintenance* by John Carruthers (Alfred Music).

Section 6: Practicing Tips and Inspiration

PRACTICING ON YOUR OWN

Here are some tips to help you achieve good results with your guitar practicing, nurture your creativity, and keep a supportive mindset.

How Much to Practice

This depends on your level and aspirations. The greater your aspirations, the more hours you'll want to put in so your identity as an artist can develop. If you just want to play guitar for fun or relaxation, spend less time.

Learning an instrument requires training your mind, ear, and the "muscle memory" and dexterity of your hands. Practicing every day allows that process to happen so it's good to practice at least 20–30 minutes every day. If you have the will and the time to do more, great!

Pick a time of the day when you feel the most alert. Don't try to cover too many areas; pick one or two specific skills to work on. You might need to stick with some of them for several weeks, which is okay. We all have to do that, regardless of level.

Consistency Takes You Places

Always show up, even if you're uninspired. This will keep the creative channel open. Consistent playing leads you to new thoughts, experiences, and places.

Build on Your Strengths: Essential Skills for a Rock Guitarist

If you're a more experienced guitarist, write your musical strengths and weaknesses in two separate columns on a piece of paper. Be honest with yourself! You'll be updating and revising this list, continually.

Your strengths might include things like "a knack for writing great riffs." Maybe your weaker spots are "stumbling when playing a fast line," or "giving up easily." You want to build on your strengths, but tackle the weaknesses that matter.

Essential skills for a rock guitarist include:

- A great ear (including the ability to figure out songs by ear).
- A solid sense of rhythm and good left- and right-hand technique so you can express your ideas without physical limitations.
- The ability to play well with singers and other musicians.
- The ability to listen.

Musical personality and style are important factors, too, but they can be developed a bit later.

Photo by Norman Seeff

"There is only one word of wisdom to give: Practice! Practice! Practice!"

Nancy Wilson, *guitarist, singer, songwriter (Heart)*

Keep Your Left Hand Strong

Rock guitar, with all its barre chords and string bending, requires a strong left hand. It's easy to scoff at guitar shops selling "grip training" devices that claim to strengthen your hands, until you hear your buzzy barre chords in a recording situation. Some women (including this author) have tiny hands and these devices can be helpful.

Another thing that'll keep your left hand strong is playing the rhythm guitar examples, soloing scales, and licks in this book. Be careful to pace yourself, though, and don't overdo it!

Play Along with Records

Play along with recordings of your favorite artists. You'll learn a lot by trying to keep up with their pace. Notice what the drummer and bass player are doing. Pay attention to the guitarist and notice if they are playing any cool fills. Decide which scale sounds best for the solo: major, minor, minor pentatonic or some other scale. You'll build your skills and confidence in a fun way.

Practice Through Composing

Playing scales and technical exercises are very useful for strengthening your hands and improving technique, but try to put what you're learning to use in a song. For example, take a legato exercise and use it to write an intro riff. Practicing through composing expands your creativity and teaches you how to *really* play your guitar. Many musicians develop their unique style this way.

The Metronome—Your Percussion Buddy

A lot of people hate practicing with a metronome. It gets much more fun if you act as if the metronome is your percussion buddy. Try to *groove* with the click. The steadier your time, the better your rhythm and lead guitar playing will feel to you *and* your band mates and audience. We humans have strong physical and emotional responses to good rhythm.

Imagine the Groove Before You Play

Before you play, just listen to the click. Imagine what your rhythm guitar part or lick will sound like with a great groove, perfectly aligned with the click. Once your ears are "at one" with the click and you *feel* the beat, start playing. Always imagine what the groove sounds like in your mind before playing.

Record Yourself

Always record your practice sessions and listen back. Also, record video of some of your practice sessions if you can. The recording doesn't lie. It's your ally and will reveal bad posture, if you're not breathing while you're practicing, if you need to slow down the metronome one click, or check your fingering or picking technique. It will also show you when you've really nailed a part, and why.

Isolate Target Issues

Don't always practice a song or solo from start to finish—it can be a waste of time. Zoom in on a few bars. Play one bar before the problem area, the part you're having trouble with, and then the bar after. You'll get more accomplished.

"I was persistent in figuring stuff out, and any time I learned something new, I would write something."

Ann Klein, *guitarist, mandolin/dobro/lap steel player, singer, composer (Ani DiFranco, Joan Osborne, various Broadway shows, solo artist)*

PRACTICING WITH OTHER MUSICIANS

Get Your Gear Ready Before Rehearsal Time

If you have a rehearsal time at 7:00 PM, you want to be in the rehearsal room at 6:30 or 6:45 PM to plug in your amp, get your guitar out of your case, tune up and—if you have pedals—get your pedal sounds turned on and dialed in. That way, others don't have to wait for you. At 7:00 PM, everybody should be ready to play.

Have a Purpose for Each Rehearsal

Decide beforehand what you want to accomplish at your next rehearsal to make it more productive. For example, you could plan to do something like make the section transitions of a song tighter before you record it next month, or create an ending for the live version of a song, or decide on a key for a song in-the-making, or sharpen your improvisation skills by jamming at the start of rehearsal.

Things to Avoid at Rehearsals

Lateness. Instrumental noodling. Volume wars (where everyone gradually gets louder). Endless chatting/discussions (save that for band meetings outside of rehearsal). Crankiness. Blaming. Learning your song parts (do it at home). Playing instrumental parts that clash with the lead vocals. Drugs.

Rehearsing to a Click

Being tight isn't just a drummer's sole responsibility; it's the whole band's. If you're preparing a show or recording, try to rehearse every song to a click track. Plug in a metronome or drum machine to the PA system so that everybody can hear the click through the speakers. Playing to a click will feel frustrating at times, but it'll make you rock solid as a band.

Two more tips that make you play better: 1) Listen to the other musicians 2) Breathe!

Record Your Rehearsals and Shows

Always record your rehearsals and shows. Video record them, too, if you can. Listen back and watch for things like transitions, intros/endings, if you're all listening to each other, if you're rushing, if the key is right for the vocals, if a solo's too long, and so on.

EVERYONE'S PATH IS UNIQUE

Overnight success stories about rock stars are usually fabricated by media. The true stories are less glamorous and more complex. Musicians become successful not only because of their talent but because they work very hard, are very persistent, believe in their talent, might have a unique style, might be good at meeting new people, aren't so sensitive about what others say that it derails them, and they've developed a circle of peers and friends. And often the truth is as plain as Ani DiFranco put it: "I played one gig and then I played another one."

Don't belittle your talents and opportunities because they don't look like someone else's. Everyone's path is completely unique, which makes it so much cooler.

Effort Goes Further than Talent

There are very talented people who procrastinate and never realize their dreams, and there are mediocre artists who get very far because they work very hard. Luckily, there are also talented people who work hard. But the key is—work hard!

Don't Listen to Negativity

People can hold themselves back for decades because of a mindless remark someone made in two seconds. Don't listen to negativity from anybody. Hang out with people who genuinely believe in you and want you to be happy. You can't hide out and just play alone in your room. Get out and build a support system of friends and artists. Play with other people. Every human being needs community. Interacting with others—artists and non-artists—will give you fresh new ideas.

TIPS IF YOU'RE UNINSPIRED

Your relationship with the guitar and music is life-long. As with any relationship, you have to nurture it so it grows and doesn't get stale. Every musician has felt stuck or uninspired at times, but there are some tried-and-true ways to help get out of a rut:

1. See and hear live music

2. Listen to and play music of a different genre than your own

3. Explore a different art form (cooking, T-shirt designing...anything!)

4. Do something that isn't typically you

5. Take a lesson from a master musician

6. Surround yourself with really creative people: see them at work, read biographies about them, tap into their mindsets and ideas

7. Write a song on a different instrument

8. Get out and see the world: go on short road trips or go abroad

9. Get out of your head and exercise (gym, dance, yoga... try it all)

10. Reconnect with why you got excited by music in the first place

On the next page, I'll share an essential listening list of albums by groundbreaking, amazing female electric guitarists. After that, Appendix A will show you how to figure out songs by ear and play in alternate tunings.

If you're stopping here, I hope you enjoyed this book and that it spurred a lot of creative ideas in you. Pass on what you've learned to others; it will make *you* a better musician. I wish you the greatest success, happiness and fulfillment in your guitar playing, music adventures and life!

Rock on!

Section 7: Inspiration: Essential Listening

Memphis Minnie (1933-1937)........... Hoodoo Lady (1991)

Sister Rosetta Tharpe............................ The Gospel of the Blues (2003)

Peggy "Lady Bo" Jones.......................... Aztek (1961)

Barbara Lynn .... You'll Lose a Good Thing (1963)

Fanny .... Fanny (1970)

Bonnie Raitt.. Bonnie Raitt (1971)

Joni Mitchell .... Hejira (1976)

The Runaways.. The Runaways (1976)

Heart... Dreamboat Annie (1976)

The Slits .... Cut (1979)

Pretenders.. Pretenders (1980)

Girlschool .... Demolition (1980)

Joan Jett & The Blackhearts................. I Love Rock N' Roll (1981)

The Go-Go's.. Beauty and the Beat (1981)

The Bangles .... All Over the Place (1984)

Sleater-Kinney....................................... Dig Me Out (1987)

Lita Ford .... Lita (1988)

Vixen .... Vixen (1988)

Jessie Mae Hemphill.............................. Feelin' Good (1987)

Cordell Jackson...................................... The Split (1989)

Wendy & Lisa.. Eroica (1990)

Jennifer Batten...................................... Above Below and Beyond (1992)

L7 .... Bricks Are Heavy (1992)

Babes in Toyland.................................Fontanelle (1992)

PJ Harvey ....Rid of Me (1993)

Debbie Davies.....................................Picture This (1993)

The Breeders......................................Last Splash (1993)

Phantom Blue......................................Built to Perform (1994)

Sonic Youth..Washing Machine (1995)

Hole ....Celebrity Skin (1998)

Drain S.T.H...Freaks of Nature (1999)

Sue Foley..Young Girl Blues (2000)

Sahara Hotnights ....Jennie Bomb (2001)

Deborah Coleman................................Soul Be It (2002)

The Donnas ....Gold Medal (2004)

Susan Tedeschi....................................Back to the River (2008)

Felicia Collins/Bitchslap.......................I'm in the Mood for Dancing (EP) (2008)

Joanne Shaw Taylor ....White Sugar (2009)

Lori Linstruth/Guilt Machine ....On This Perfect Day (EP) (2009)

Kaki King..Junior (2010)

Marnie Stern......................................Marnie Stern (2010)

St. Vincent ....Strange Mercy (2011)

Those Dancing Days ....Daydreams & Nightmares (2011)

Joanna Connor ....Live 24 (2011)

Wild Flag..Wild Flag (2011)

Rosie Flores ....Working Girl's Guitar (2012)

Janet Robin..Everything Has Changed (2012)

Orianthi...Heaven in This Hell (2013)

Ana Popovic.......................................Can You Stand the Heat? (2013)

Are there other great female rock/blues guitarists around the world that we should know about?
Go to womensroadtorockguitar.com and tell us!

Appendix A: Advanced Concepts

HOW TO FIGURE OUT SONGS BY EAR

The feeling of accomplishment you get when you've figured out a tune by ear is amazing! Developing this skill will also help you play more efficiently with other musicians. You won't need to depend on others to show you every chord of a song—you'll be able to hear it yourself, which saves rehearsal time (and the drummer won't get bored). The formal word for figuring out a song is *transcribing*.

Five Steps to Figuring Out the Chords to a Song

Try this five-step approach with every song you hear. Start off with just one section of a song, such as the chorus.

1. Listen to the guitar part in the chosen section closely. Rewind and replay as much as necessary.

2. Identify the root note of the first chord by playing different notes on your 6th string until you've found the perfect match. Write down the name of that note. Repeat this process with the rest of the chords.

3. Once you've identified and written down the root note of each chord, play along with the track, but don't play any chords yet. Just play the single root notes, as if you were a bass player. Correct any notes that you misheard the first time.

4. Convert the root notes into power chords and play along with the track again. Correct any notes that you may have misheard previously.

5. Now, listen to the first chord and figure out if it's major or minor. Match it with a barred or open major or minor chord on your guitar. Repeat this process with the other chords until you've transcribed the entire section.

Transcribe Four Bars

Track 187 Listen to the track and see if you can figure out this four-bar chord progression. First, note how many chords are there in each bar. Then, determine the names of the chords and decide which are major or minor. Fill in the chord names in the blank measures below. You'll find the correct answer in the upside-down text below at the bottom of the page, but don't cheat—give your ears a chance to practice!

bpm = 110

> "Having taught myself to play the guitar by ear, I would sit and listen to all my favorite guitarists—Jimmy Page, Jimi Hendrix, Ritchie Blackmore, Johnny Winter, Michael Schenker—or anything that struck me as musically interesting, even violin parts…
>
> I used my mother and father's old record player, and used to push the needle back over the grooves in the record so I could hear the solos and riffs over and over. I would start from the beginning, learn the riffs or solos note by note until I worked my way through the entire solo.
>
> Learning by ear still pays off. As of today, I can hear a guitar part and know exactly how and what is being played."
>
> **Lita Ford**, guitarist, singer, songwriter (solo artist, The Runaways)

Answers for Track 187:

C–Am | F–G | C–Dm | F–G

ALTERNATE TUNINGS

When a guitar's strings are tuned in any other way than the standard E–A–D–G–B–E, it's in an *alternate tuning*. There are endless varieties of alternate tunings in rock, from lowering just the 6th string to re-tuning several or all of the strings to sound a chord when you strum across them (an *open tuning*). We'll explore just a few common examples. Keep your electronic guitar tuner on hand for this!

NOTE: As you change tunings, be aware that the chord shapes you're accustomed to are going to change. How drastically they'll change depends on how many strings you've re-tuned, and how much.

Drop Tunings

A *drop tuning* is usually a tuning where the 6th string is lowered a half step or more. But it can also refer to more strings being lowered.

All Strings Down a Half Step to E♭

Many rock artists tune all six strings down a half step to E♭–A♭–D♭–G♭–B♭–E♭. Sometimes this can help to better match a singer's vocal range, make string bending easier, or create a heavier, darker sound.

 PUMPKIN BULLET

Track 188

Let's tune down to E♭ and play something in the style of Smashing Pumpkins' "Bullet with Butterfly Wings."

⑥=E♭ ③=G♭
⑤=A♭ ②=B♭
④=D♭ ①=E♭

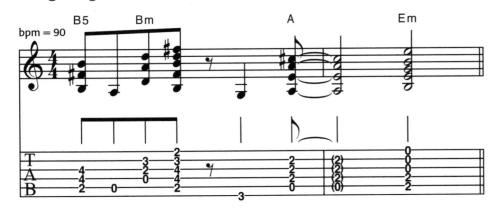

 Electronic tuners sometimes feature altered notes as sharps instead of flats, so when you tune your guitar down to E♭, here's how the string names could show up on your display:

⑥=D♯ ③=F♯
⑤=G♯ ②=A♯
④=C♯ ①=D♯

Sonic Youth uses some of their unusual tunings for just a song or two, so they bring a lot of different guitars on tour. Gov't Mule's guitarist Warren Haynes has guitars designated for drop tunings and slide guitar tunings, while Ani DiFranco tours with acoustic guitars that are set up to accommodate heavier string gauges and lower tunings.

Drop D

In *Drop D* tuning, the 6th string is lowered a whole step to D. Many metal bands, including Shadows Fall and Avenged Sevenfold, use this tuning since it makes it easy to play very fast power chords (laying your finger across the two strings on the same fret). You'll also hear it in Metallica's "Sad But True," Nirvana's "Come As You Are," and in songs by Muse, Tool, and Soundgarden.

 OUTRAGED

Track 189

Let's tune the 6th string down to D and play a riff in the style of Rage Against the Machine's "Killing in the Name."

For even lower drop tunings, many metal bands use seven-string guitars. In extreme cases, some bands will even play eight-string guitars and lower them three steps.

Guitarists who play in different alternate tunings often designate specific guitars to certain tunings. If they constantly change string tensions, it puts a lot of stress on the guitar. Sometimes they'll need to change to heavier or lighter strings.

Contemporary metal guitarists, who often drop their strings down several steps, need heavier strings because standard .09 gauge strings feel as loose as rubber bands in dropped tunings.

If you change string gauges, it's important to take the guitar to a luthier/guitar repair shop for a setup, so that the intonation gets re-adjusted for the new string gauge and tension.

* Quarter-note triplets are played as three in the time of two quarter notes, or one half note.

Open Chord Tunings

These tunings create the sound of a specific chord when you strum across the open strings. They're very popular in slide guitar, since it makes playing chord progressions like I–IV–V very easy—one simply barres all six strings on the desired fret, and you've got a chord!

Open G Tuning

If you tune your guitar to D–G–D–G–B–D (starting with the 6th string) and then strum across the open strings, you'll get the sound of a G major chord.

For an R&B-influenced band like The Rolling Stones, the open G tuning is a major part of their sound. You can hear it in "Brown Sugar" and "Start Me Up."

 SHAKE HER UP

Track 190

Pull out your electronic tuner, tune to a open G tuning, and let's play this riff in the style of The Rolling Stones' "Start Me Up."

⑥ =D ③=G
⑤ =G ②=B
④ =D ①=D

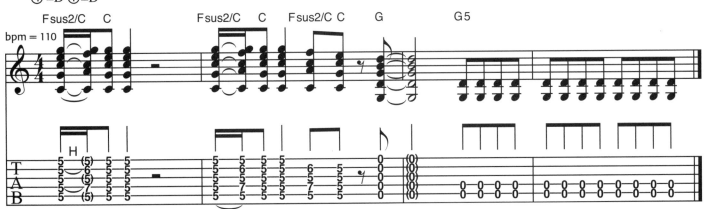

Open E Tuning

If you tune your guitar to E–B–E–G♯–B–E, you'll get the sound of an E major chord.

This will get you the right sound for The Black Crowes' "She Talks to Angels" and many songs by blues pioneers like Memphis Minnie and Robert Johnson.

NOTE: Since you'll be raising three of the six strings, you might want to use a lighter string gauge (.10). Don't leave the guitar in this tuning—you need a pro setup for that.

 GIRL HEARS ANGELS

Track 191

Let's tune to an open E tuning and play in the style of "She Talks to Angels."

⑥ =E ③=G♯
⑤ =B ②=B
④ =E ①=E

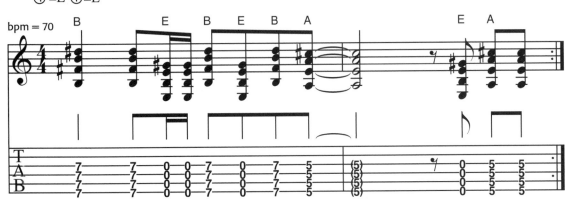

Appendix B: Quick Review of the Basics

TUNING YOUR GUITAR

It's wise to learn how to tune your guitar by ear, and not rely solely on an electronic tuner to do the job. If the battery unexpectedly dies before a band rehearsal or during a show, you'll be forced to tune by ear. Try to tune at least one string by ear when you're practicing, and then work your way up to tuning all six strings that way. Before you know it, you'll start hearing when your guitar sounds "off" and needs tuning.

Strings will be wrapped around the tuning pegs differently depending on the type of headstock design your electric guitar has. Turning the tuning peg so that it tightens the string will raise the pitch. If you turn the tuning peg the opposite way, it will loosen the string and lower the pitch.

NOTE: New strings will take a while to stretch properly. In the meantime, they'll go out of tune often. Make sure you play your guitar a lot (to help the strings stretch) and tune it often. This way, the strings will stretch and become more stable more quickly.

Tuning the Guitar by Ear

Tune the 6th string to an E with your electronic tuner and then proceed without the tuner as follows:

Play the 6th string, 5th fret to get the pitch of the 5th string (A). Now play the open 5th string and adjust it to match the 6th string.

Play the 5th string, 5th fret to get the pitch of the 4th string (D). Now play the open 4th string and adjust it to match the 5th string.

Play the 4th string, 5th fret to get pitch of the 3rd string (G). Now play the open 3rd string and adjust it to match the 4th string.

Play the 3rd string, 4th fret to get the pitch of the 2nd string (B). Now play the open 2nd string and adjust it to match the 3rd string.

Play the 2nd string, 5th fret to get the pitch of the 1st string (E). Now play the open 1st string and adjust it to match the 2nd string.

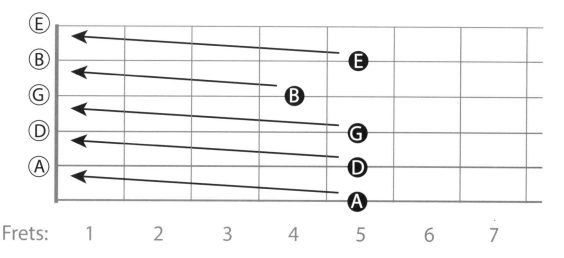

Tuning with the CD

Track 1   To tune while listening to the CD, listen to the directions and match each of your strings to the corresponding pitches.

MUSIC AND GUITAR FUNDAMENTALS

Before you dive into Section 2, make sure you check out this review of the basics. Here, we'll quickly cover the names of the strings, the notes on the strings from the open string to the 3rd fret, the open position chords, how to read basic rhythmic notation, count time, and measures and time signatures.

The basics of reading TAB and rhythmic notation are covered on page 14, and reading chord diagrams is covered on page 9. Some of what follows will have been covered earlier in the book, but a little repetition never hurts when it comes to learning! If you feel that this review is going way too fast for you, check out the books *Teach Yourself to Play Rock Guitar,* or *Girls Guitar Method 1* (Alfred Music).

The Musical Alphabet

The musical alphabet in Western music consists of only seven letters:

A, B, C, D, E, F, G

After G, the alphabet repeats, starting with A again. When you play a scale, no matter what note-name you start from, the notes continue in alphabetical order.

Exercise: Name the seven notes in the musical alphabet forward and backward.

Forward: ___ ___ ___ ___ ___ ___ ___

Backward: ___ ___ ___ ___ ___ ___ ___

The Names of the Six Strings

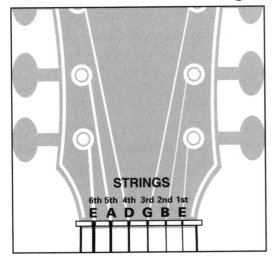

The thinnest string—the one closest to the floor while holding your guitar, is the 1st string. It's also the string that is the highest in pitch. The thickest and lowest sounding string is the 6th string. From 1st to 6th, the strings are named E–B–G–D–A–E.

There are many different acronyms that people have made up to help them remember the names of the strings. Starting from the 1st string, here's one example:

"**E**very **B**eautiful **G**uitar **D**eserves **A**mps **E**very Day"

EXERCISE: Create your own acronym for the six strings, starting from the 1st string, and write it here:

_____

The 1st and 2nd Strings

Notes on the 1st String (E)

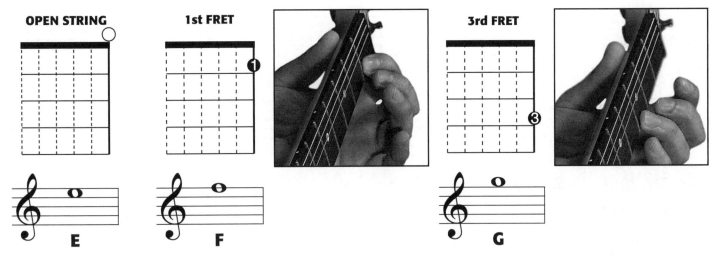

 Playing with E, F, and G on the 1st String

Track 192
bpm = 70

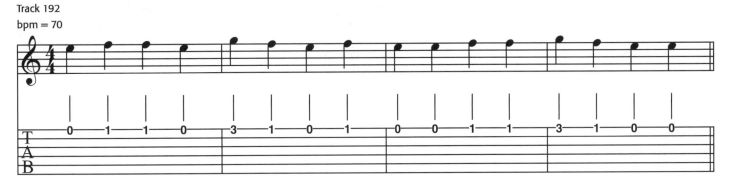

EXERCISE: Write the names of the notes underneath each note in the example above.

Notes on the 2nd String (B)

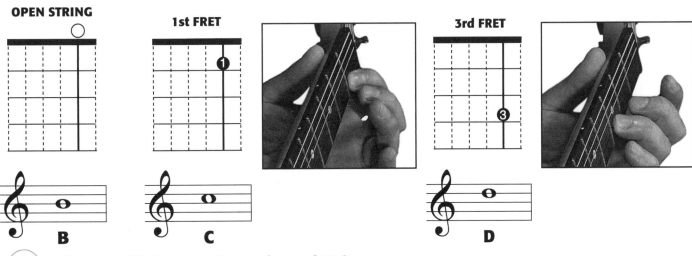

 Playing with B, C, and D on the 2nd String

Track 193
bpm = 70

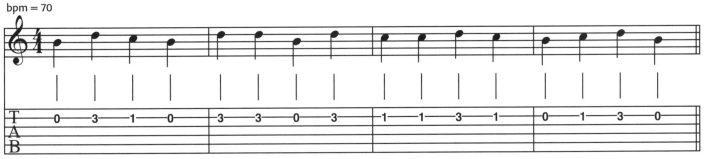

Playing with B, C, D, E, F, and G

Track 194   Now let's combine all the notes you've learned on the 1st and 2nd strings.

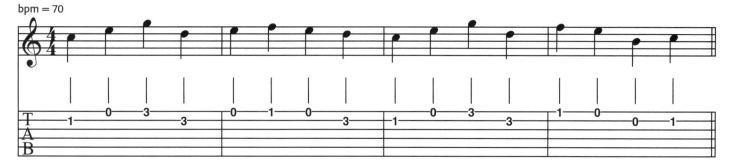

The 3rd and 4th Strings

Notes on the 3rd String (G)

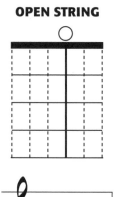

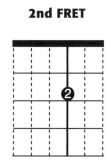

EXERCISE: When you have learned to play all of the examples on this page, write the names of the notes underneath.

 Playing G and A on the 3rd String

Track 195

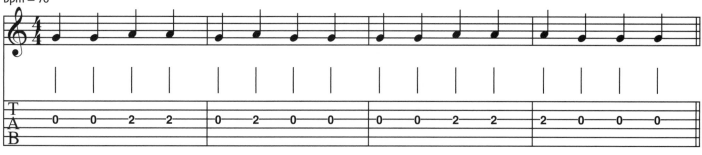

 Playing the Notes You've Learned So far

Track 196   Let's play the notes you've learned on the 1st, 2nd, and 3rd strings. Hey! That's eight notes!

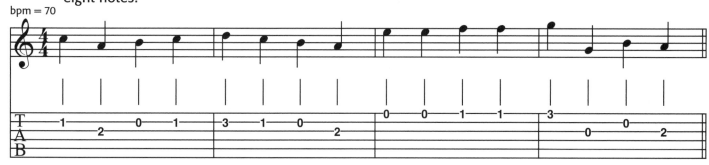

Notice that you've learned to read G in two places. These two G's are said to be one *octave* apart. There's actually a third G that's one octave (eight notes) lower. We'll play it soon.

Notes on the 4th String (D)

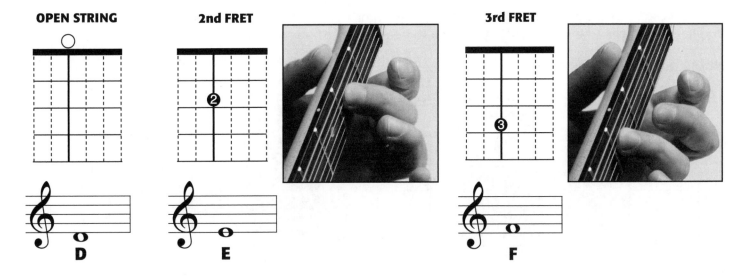

OPEN STRING — D **2nd FRET** — E **3rd FRET** — F

 Playing on D, E and F on the 4th String

Track 197

bpm = 70

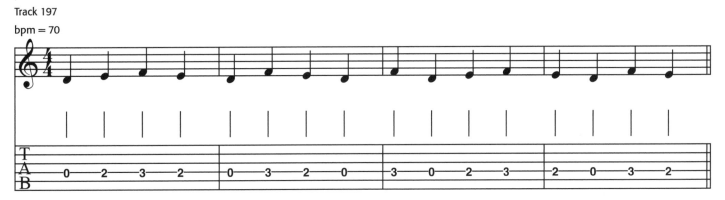

 Playing on the 1st, 2nd, 3rd, and 4th Strings

Track 198 Now let's play the notes of the E, B, G, and D strings

bpm = 70

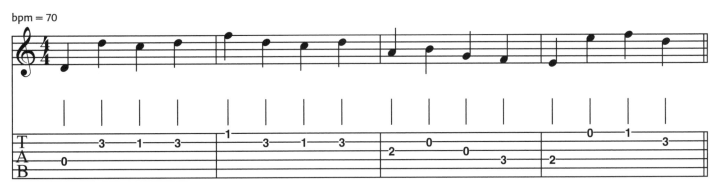

Exercise: Write the names of the notes under the music in the example above. Notice that you can now play E, F, and G in two different octaves.

Notes on the 5th and 6th Strings

The low notes on these bottom strings are important for playing many rock guitar *riffs*. A riff is a catchy instrumental part of a song. Listen to "Smoke on the Water" by Deep Purple and "Smells Like Teen Spirit" by Nirvana to hear some famous rock riffs.

Notes on the 5th String (A)

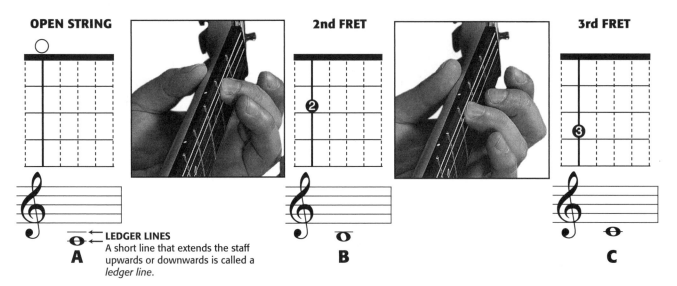

LEDGER LINES
A short line that extends the staff upwards or downwards is called a *ledger line*.

Track 199

Playing with A, B, and C on the 5th String

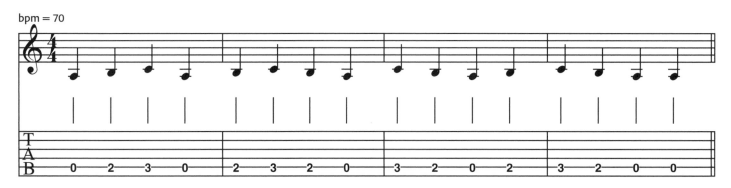

QUIZ: Which seven notes do you know how to play in two different octaves?

__ __ __ __ __ __ __

Quiz Answer: Which seven notes do you know how to play in two different octaves?

G F E D C B A

And Finally, The Notes on the 6th String (E)

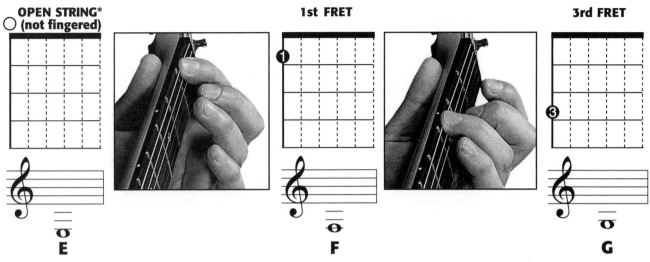

OPEN STRING* (not fingered) — **E**

1st FRET — **F**

3rd FRET — **G**

Playing with E, F, and G on the 6th String

Track 200

bpm = 70

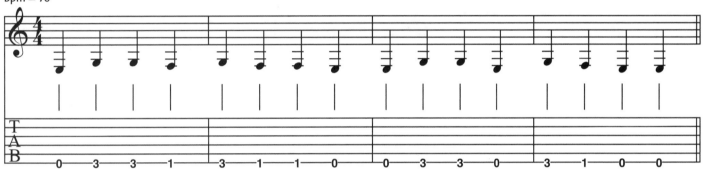

A Hoochie Coochie Kind of Riff

Track 201
Now let's make some music! We're going to play a bluesy rock riff using the notes on the 4th, 5th, and 6th strings.

bpm = 70

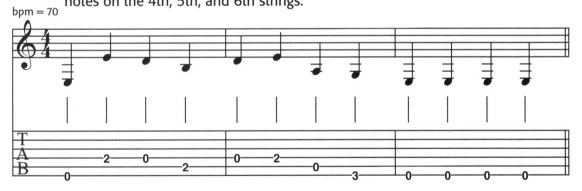

Here's your chance to get creative. Write your own riff! Use notes from the 5th and 6th strings. Feel free to also include notes from the 4th string, too, if you like. Then, write the names of the notes underneath the music.

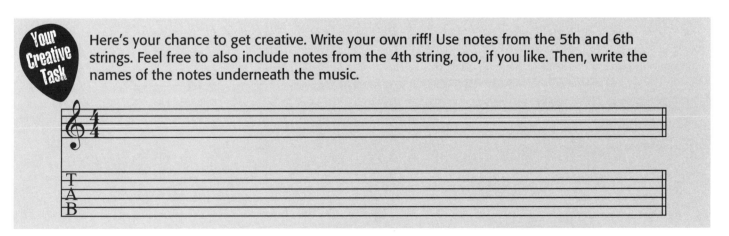

All the Notes You've Learned

Track 202 Congratulations! You've learned how to play seventeen notes! Before we wrap
up with a song using all these notes, here they are in a quick review:

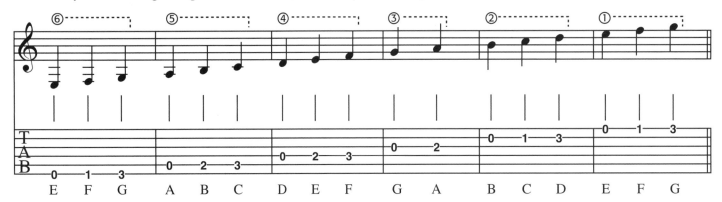

 # THE GRAND FINALE SONG: "HIGH AND LOW ECHOES"

Track 203

bpm = 70

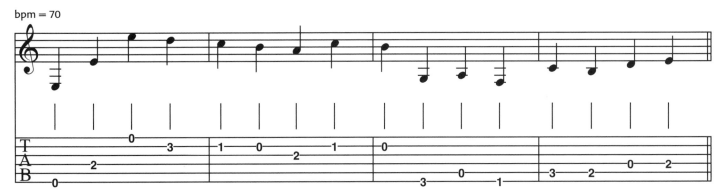

> Surely this review must have gone by with the speed of lightning. Nobody
> would, or should, ever expect a beginner to nail all seventeen notes right away.
>
> If you feel that you need more work on these notes, please check out the books
> *Teach Yourself To Play Rock Guitar,* or *Girls Guitar Method 1*, both of which use
> both TAB and standard music notation. Pick one and take your time with it by learning
> the notes at your own pace. It will also teach you how to play some basic chords.
>
> Don't rush through the fundamentals—this book will be here, waiting for you when
> you're ready!

THE OPEN CHORDS

Here's a review of some very common major, minor, and 7th chords, including the F major chord. These are *open chords*. "Open" refers to the open strings that are included in most of the chords on this page. These chords are all located in the first three frets of the fingerboard. If you're unfamiliar with these chords, please check out *Alfred's Basic Guitar Chord Chart* (Alfred Music).

Major Chords

Track 204

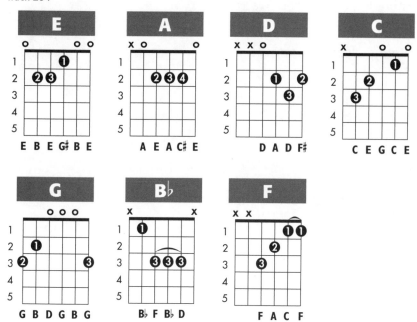

To play the F chord, your 1st finger will lay across the 1st and 2nd strings at the 1st fret. This is a *barre*. The F chord is a common transition into learning full barre chords over five or six strings, which is covered in Section 2. You'll also learn how to play the F chord there in three gradual steps (page 39).

Minor Chords

Track 205   Minor chords are said to have a darker and sadder sound when compared to major chords.

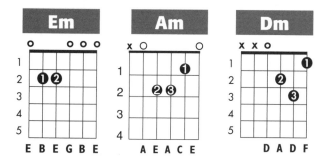

7th Chords

Track 206   Notice the similarities between the 7th chord and major chord shapes.

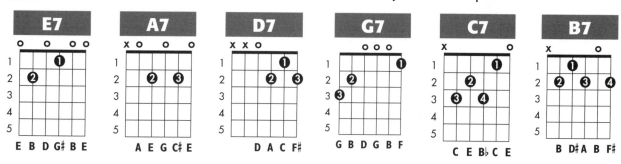

COUNTING TIME: HOW TO READ BASIC RHYTHMIC NOTATION

Many guitarists read music and many don't. You don't have to read music in order to play guitar. Many of us learn to play by listening to records or tracks of our favorite artists, and figuring out the parts by ear. But most musicians who play by ear still have a grasp of basic rhythmic terms, such as the length of notes and time signatures.

Three Benefits of Knowing Basic Rhythmic Notation

You will:

- Read and play the strum patterns in this book much easier.
- Figure out songs and guitar parts so much faster.
- Be better and quicker at articulating rhythmic ideas for songs to your band members.

The Lengths of the Notes

Note Values

As you know, the location of a note relative to the staff tells us its pitch (how high or how low it is). The duration, or value, is indicated by its shape.

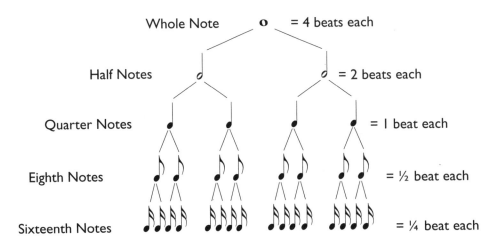

Time Signatures

Every piece of music has numbers at the beginning that tell us how to count time. The top number represents the number of beats per measure. The bottom number represents the type of note receiving one count.

4 ← Four beats per measure
4 ← Quarter note ♩ = one beat

3 ← Three beats per measure
4 ← Quarter note ♩ = one beat

Sometimes a 𝄴 is written in place of $\frac{4}{4}$.

This is called *common time* because it is one of the most widely used time signatures.

6 ← Six beats per measure
8 ← Eighth note ♪ = one beat

Subdivisions—Beamed Notes

Notes that are shorter than one beat in duration (eighth notes, sixteenth notes, and eighth-note triplets) are sometimes called *subdivisions* because they divide a beat into smaller parts. Multiple eighth notes and sixteenth notes are often connected with *beams*. You'll see a lot of beamed notes in rhythm strums and lead guitar parts.

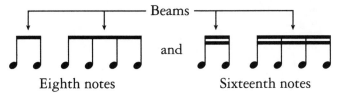

How to Count Subdivisions

Track 207 There are various ways to count eighth notes, sixteenth notes, and triplets which make them easier to feel and understand. Listen to the track as you read the notes below:

Counting Eighth Notes

Counting Sixteenth Notes

Counting Eighth-Note Triplets

There are two popular ways to count eighth-note triplets.

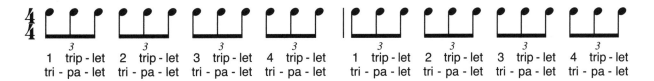

Ties

A *tie* is a curved line that connects two or more notes of the same pitch. When two notes are tied, the second one is not played; rather, the value is added to the first note.

Hold D for 5 beats.

Dotted Notes

A dot increases the length of a note by one half.

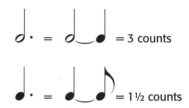

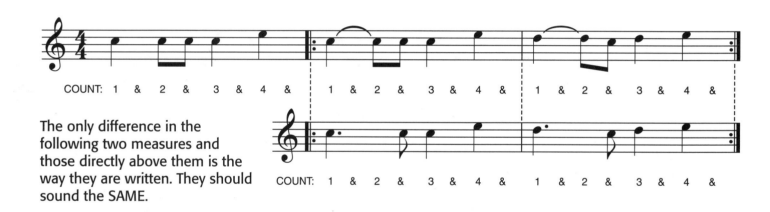

The only difference in the following two measures and those directly above them is the way they are written. They should sound the SAME.